A Syntropic Model of Consciousness

Antonella Vannini

www.sintropia.it

CONTENTS

ACKNOWLEDGMENTS

This book was inspired by the work of professor Luigi Fantappiè and his 1941 *"Unitary Theory of the Physical and Biological World."*

I want to express my gratitude to Ulisse Di Corpo for his precious help and collaboration and to Robert Jahn and Brenda Dunne of the International Consciousness Research Laboratories (Princeton)

PROLOGUE

In the introduction to The Conscious Mind David Chalmers states that:

"Consciousness is the biggest mystery. It may be the largest outstanding obstacle in our quest for scientific understanding of the universe. The science of physics is not yet complete, but it is well understood; the science of biology has removed many ancient mysteries surrounding the nature of life. There are gaps in our understanding of these fields, but they do not seem intractable. We have a sense of what a solution to these problems might look like; we just need to get the details right. Even in the science of the mind, much progress has been made. Recent work in cognitive science and neuroscience is leading us to a better understanding of human behavior and of the processes that drive it. We do not have many detailed theories of cognition, to be sure, but the details cannot be too far off. Consciousness, however, is as perplexing as it ever was. It still seems utterly mysterious that the causation of behavior should be accompanied by a subjective inner life. We have good reason to believe that consciousness arises from physical systems such as brains, but we have little idea how it arises, or why it exists at all. How could a physical systems such as a brain also be an experiencer? Why should there be something it is like to be such a system? Present-day scientific theories hardly touch the really difficult questions about consciousness. We do not just lack a detailed theory; we are entirely in the dark about how consciousness fits into the natural order."

Chalmers divides the problems of consciousness into:

1. The *easy problem*, which deals with the study of neurobiological models of consciousness. Considering the enormous progresses of science it is relatively simple to find neural correlates of the conscious experiences. The easy problems largely deal with the functioning of the brain in the way it transmits and reads sensory signals, in the processing of information, in the control of behavior, in the mechanisms underlying intelligence and memory, in the capability of reproducing verbal accounts, etc. Nevertheless, according to Chalmers, this approach does not

1

explain the subjective qualities that consciousness has for the subject; in other words this approach is not able to answer the problem of the phenomenal consciousness.

2. The *hard problem* which deals with the explanation of the qualitative and subjective aspects of consciousness, which escape a physicalistic and materialistic analysis.

Chalmers says that:

"The really hard problem of consciousness is the problem of experience. When we think and perceive, there is a whir of information-processing, but there is also a subjective aspect. As Nagel has put it, there is something it is like to be conscious organism. This subjective aspect is experience."

Chalmers affirms that easy problems are easy because all that it is needed is to find the mechanisms which allow to explain them, making them compatible with the laws of classical physics. The problem of consciousness is different from the easy problem since, even when all the main functions are explained according to cause-effect processes, it is impossible to arrive at the explanation of consciousness, in the term of subjective experience, according to the laws of classical physics.

In the first chapter of this work models suggested by Antonio Damasio, Gerald Edelman and Francisco Varela are described. These models try to explain consciousness using the principles of classical physics.

In the second chapter the principles of Quantum mechanics (QM) and its main interpretations will be introduced in order to describe the models of consciousness which are based on QM.

In the 1930s, while the field of psychology was dominated by behaviorism, which did not consider consciousness a field for scientific investigation, the most important interpretations of Quantum Mechanics were using consciousness in order to explain the strange behaviors of the sub-atomic world. For example, according to the Copenhagen interpretation the wave function collapses into a particle only when a conscious observation is performed through an act of measurement. In this interpretation consciousness itself creates matter, and it is not matter which creates consciousness.

Quantum models of consciousness described in chapter 2 can be divided in three main categories:

1. models which assume that consciousness creates reality and that consciousness is an immanent property of reality;
2. models which link consciousness to the probabilistic properties of quantum mechanics;
3. models which attribute consciousness to a principle of order of quantum mechanics.

Analyzing the quantum models of consciousness which belong to the first category a tendency towards mysticism can be observed. All these models start from the Copenhagen interpretation of quantum mechanics and assume that consciousness itself determines reality. These models try to describe the creation of reality as a consequence of panpsychism, and assume that consciousness is an immanent property which precedes the formation of reality. The concept of panpsychism is explicitly used by most of the authors of this category. These assumptions cannot be falsified or tested in an experiment.

Analyzing the quantum models of consciousness which belong to the second category, also in this case, it is impossible to falsify the assumptions or test the models using experiments, as they consider consciousness to be linked to a realm, for example that of the Planck's constant, which cannot be observed by modern science.

Analyzing the third group of models which attribute consciousness to principles of order which have been already discovered and used for physical applications (laser, superconductors, etc.) it is possible to imagine experimental tests which could falsify them. However it is important to note that many of these models require conditions which are not compatible with biological systems. The order principles on which most of these models are based require extreme physical conditions such as, for example, absolute zero temperatures (-273 C°).

Using together the criteria of scientific falsification and the criteria of biological compatibility only two models, one suggested by Luigi Fantappiè (1942) and the other suggested by Chris King (2003), survive this selection. It is interesting to note that these models are not pure quantum mechanical models, as they both originate from the generalization of Schrödinger's wave equation (quantum mechanics) with special relativity.

In conclusion, it seems that all the models of consciousness which start from quantum mechanics cannot be translated into experiments, either because they cannot be falsified or because they are not compatible with the requirements of biology. The only two models which offer the possibility to be translated into experiments are those which unite quantum mechanics with special relativity.

The third chapter describes in more details King and Fantappiè's models, while the fourth chapter is dedicated to the relation between causality and time. The understanding of this relation is fundamental for the understanding of the models of consciousness which are based on the principles of quantum mechanics and special relativity.

In chapters 5 to 8 four experimental studies, designed in order to verify the assumptions of King and Fantappiè's models, are described and their results are discussed.

1

CONSCIOUSNESS
ACCORDING TO CLASSICAL PHYSICS

Many authors are interested in and are studying consciousness and mental states, and there is a wide variety of positions ranging from models based on classical physics (for example the models suggested by Paul Churchland, Antonio Damasio, Daniel Dennett, Gerald Edelman, Francisco Varela and John Searle), to models based on the properties of Quantum Mechanics, such as the dual nature of matter (particle and wave), the collapse of the wave function, non-locality and the unified field (John Eccles, Stuart Hameroff, Roger Penrose and Chris King). Nevertheless an authentic understanding of mental phenomena seems to be still far away.

In this chapter Antonio Damasio, Gerald Edelman and Francisco Varela's models of consciousness, based on classical physics, are described.

These models show a different attitude towards localization: Damasio suggests neural sites in which consciousness could take place, Edelman suggests that consciousness is a global process of all the brain and Varela considers consciousness as a distributed quality of all the organism and of the interaction of the organism with the environment.

1.1 Consciousness according to Damasio

Many authors link consciousness to cognition and thinking, while Damasio links consciousness to emotions and feelings. Damasio's motto is: "*I feel therefore I am.*" The importance of emotions was clearly stated in *Descarte's Error* (Damasio, 1994); in this book Damasio describes the importance of emotions in order to decide advantageously.

It is necessary to clarify the meaning that the words emotions and feelings have for Damasio.

Usually, in common language, no distinction between emotions and feelings is made, and these words are used practically in the same way. Damasio, instead, uses them in different ways (even if they belong to the same processes):

1. *Emotions* are a collection of chemical and neural responses, which form a configuration and have the function of leading the organism to choose advantageously. Emotions are relative to the life of the organism, of its body, and the role of the organism in order to survive. The mechanisms which produce emotions are placed in a limited area of the subcortical region, starting from the encephalic trunk; these mechanisms are part of a group of structures which regulate and represent the inner states of the body and can be activated automatically, without any conscious decision. Emotions use the body as a theatre (inner milieu, visceral systems, vestibular and muscle and skeletal apparatus), and influence the way in which many brain circuits work. Emotional responses are responsible for profound changes in the body and in the brain. The collection of these changes forms the underlying substrate of neural configurations which are the feelings and the emotions (Damasio, 1999).

2. According to Damasio the mechanism of emotions results in *feelings*. Feelings translate in the language of mind the vital states of the organism: mental maps of the states of the organism. At the origin of feelings there are emotions produced by the body, made of different parts which are constantly recorded by brain structures. Feelings are the perception of a specific state of the body, to which a state of the mind can be associated. Damasio distinguishes between feeling the emotions and feeling the background. In the case of feeling the emotions Damasio says that the essence of this experience is the experience of the change which takes place at the body level and which is juxtaposed to mental maps and mental images. In other words, an emotion is felt when the variation of a body state is linked to a cognitive content. Background feelings, instead, precede feeling the emotions and originate from background body states.

Background feeling is the feeling of life itself. Background feelings corresponds to the state of the body which prevails among emotions, it is our image of the body state when it is not moved by emotions. According to Damasio, without the background feeling, the representation of the self would be disrupted.

In *The Feeling of What Happens* (Damasio, 1999) describes consciousness as the knowledge of feelings: consciousness is experienced as a feeling and, consequently, if it is experienced as a feeling it could probably be a feeling.

Damasio says that consciousness is not perceived as an image, neither as a visual, auditive, smell or taste configuration. Consciousness is not seen or heard. Consciousness has no smell or taste.

According to Damasio consciousness is a configuration constituted by the nonverbal signs of the body states.

Damasio divides consciousness into 3 levels: proto-self, nuclear self and autobiographical self.

- The proto-self

Proto-self is a collection of coherent maps, neural configurations which coincide with the basic adjustments of life. This collection of neural configurations is constantly updated and can be found in many locations of the brain at multiple levels, from the encephalic trunk to the brain cortex and in interconnected neuron structures. According to Damasio we are not conscious of the proto-self.

- The nuclear self

Damasio suggests that consciousness starts when the maps of the proto-self are changed by the interaction with an object. Nuclear consciousness arises when brain representations generate a nonverbal description, based on images, of the way in which the state of the organism is being modified by the interaction with the object. The object with which the organism interacts, can be real or recalled by memory, inside or outside the organism. The interaction with the object triggers an impulse of consciousness. Consciousness would be the consequence of these impulses and the continuity of consciousness would be the result of the constant generation of these impulses by the interaction with thousands of objects, real or recalled, which constantly modify the maps of the proto-self. More objects can interact with the organism at the same time and modify the proto-self and consciousness can arise by multiple interaction with objects.

While the proto-self is a non-conscious state, the nuclear self is the first stage of consciousness and coincides with the knowledge of feeling emotions. The biological essence of the nuclear self is the representation of a map of the proto-self which is being modified. This change is caused by the interaction with an object which modifies the perception of the inner states of the body, of the proto-self, causing emotions. The nuclear self is nonverbal and can be caused by any object. As there is always ample availability of objects, the conscious experience is continuous and it is therefore experienced as a continuous state. The mechanism of the nuclear self requires the existence of the proto-self.

Nuclear consciousness is the most simple type of consciousness and gives a sense of self to the organism in a specific moment and place ("here and now"). Nuclear consciousness is a simple biological phenomenon which has only one level of organization, it is stable during all the life of the organism, it is not exclusive only to human beings, and does not depend on memory, reasoning or language. Nuclear self-arises from the interaction of the organism with an object. It is based on the experience of changes in the organism and it is induced by the interaction with objects. The proto-self is a biological precursor of what, with the nuclear self, becomes the elusive feeling of consciousness.

The nuclear self-coincides with feelings, with the ability of the organism to feel emotions which regulate the life of the organism.

This happens when the organism processes sensory or memory information, for example when we observe a face or a landscape, or when the mind recalls an object or a specific situations and represents them as images in the process of the mind.

The model of the nuclear self is based on the following elements:

1. The organism, as a unity, is projected in brain maps, in structures which constantly inform about the inner states of the organism. Damasio calls these maps, maps of the first order.
2. Sensory and motion structures, activated by the object, are projected in the maps of the first order, which represent the organism.
3. These projections produce modifications in the maps of the organism.
4. Modifications generate maps of the second order, which represent the interaction between the organism and the object.
5. Neural configurations which are momentarily formed by the maps of the second order can be translated into images.
6. Consciousness would arise from the construction of mental images caused by the interaction of objects with the organism.
7. Both the maps of the organism and the maps of the second order are linked to the body; consequently the images which describe relations among the organism and objects are feelings.

- The autobiographical self

The first level of consciousness starts from the re-representation of the non-conscious proto-self while it is being modified by the interaction with an object. The autobiographical consciousness arises from the description of the interactions with the object: we know we exist because our narrated history shows us as actors in the interaction with the object.

Autobiographical consciousness, or extended consciousness, depends on the same mechanism as nuclear consciousness, but it connects the feeling of self to past and future events in an autobiographical narration. The self which derives from this process is a strong and robust self. It is an autobiographical self.

The autobiographical self, or extended consciousness, coincides with the higher level of consciousness. The autobiographical self is based on the ability of the person to keep track of his history. The autobiographical self is based on the autobiographical memory which is formed by implicit memories of a great number of individual experiences of the past and of the foreseen future. The autobiographical memory grows with the increase of life experiences, and can be partially changed in order to accommodate new experiences. Groups of autobiographical memories can be activated as neural configurations and become explicit in the form of images. Each time an object is recalled it generates an impulse of nuclear consciousness, this results in the autobiographical self of which we are conscious. The autobiographical self is based on experiences of the nuclear self which have been recorded in time and which can be activated and transformed into images. The autobiographical self requires the presence of a nuclear self.

Autobiographical consciousness is the most complex level of consciousness. It is a complex biological phenomena, with different levels of organization, which evolve during the history of the organism.

Neurological syndromes show that the impairment of the extended consciousness does not affect the capability of the nuclear consciousness to remain intact. On the contrary, the impairment of the nuclear consciousness destroys the higher levels of consciousness.

Extended consciousness would arise from two different types of processes:

1. The first requires the gradual accumulation of memories of a specific class of objects. Each of these autobiographical memories is then treated by our brain as an object, becoming an inducer of consciousness.
2. The second consists in keeping active, at the same time, several images which form together the autobiographical self and which define the object. The autobiographical self can take place only in

organisms which are equipped with a good sized memory and a high level of reasoning, but it does not require the use of language.

Extended consciousness arises when operational memory keeps active, simultaneously, both an object and the autobiographical self. In this process both the past which has been experienced and the future which is being expected are important. Future experiences, which are expected, have a great influence on the process of the autobiographical self. Memories of our desires and of the outcomes which we expect generate a pressure in each moment on our self.

According to Damasio, consciousness was formed in order to cope with the requirements of survival. In order to survive it is necessary to find and acquire energy and prevent all those situations which threaten the integrity of living structures. With no action, organisms like ours would not survive, because they would not find the sources of energy needed in order to renew structures and stay alive, and they would not use energy for their survival. Actions are guided by nuclear and extended consciousness and efficient actions require consciousness based on good images. Actions are at the basis of survival and their power relies on the availability of using good images, the result is that consciousness, which maximizes the efficiency of images, would provide enormous advantages for survival, leading to the natural selection of those organisms which are based on conscious processes. The big opportunity which is offered by consciousness is the link between mechanisms which regulate life and the production of images. This link constitutes a real advantage because the survival in a complex environment depends on the choice of the right action.

- Localization of consciousness

The link between behavior and brain became clear more than a century ago when Paul Broca and Carl Wernicke discovered that specific damages in areas of the left brain hemisphere caused language deficits. New techniques of investigation allow to study brain damages, with a three-dimensional reconstruction of the brain, when the patient is still alive. In this way it is now possible to study the behavior of patients with specific damages. Using this process of investigation, Damasio discovered that neural damages localized in the prefrontal regions of the brain, especially in the ventral and medial sectors and in the right parietal region, are systematically associated with decision making deficits, which are often associated with severe alterations of the perception of emotions and feelings. Family members report that it is possible to recognize an exact "before" and "after" the neurological lesion. These studies show that the reduction of emotions impairs the rational process of decision making. Emotions seem to be an essential element in the process of reasoning. Without emotions all the process of reasoning and decision making is no longer oriented towards the future.

- Localization of the proto-self

With emotions, specific regions of the brain send commands to other regions of the brain and to nearly all the regions of the body using two different ways. One is the blood circulation, in which commands are carried by molecules, chemical substances, which act on the receptors of cells which form the tissues of the body. The other is the neural networks in which commands are sent in the form of electro-chemical signals which act on the neurons, on muscular fibers and on organs (such as the surrenal gland) which can free chemical substances in the blood. The result of these chemical and neural commands is a global change in the state of the organism.

Substances such as monoamines and peptides, produced in the regions of the encephalic trunk and of the basal proencephalus, alter the modality in which brain neural circuits process the information, trigger specific behaviors and change the way in which the states of the body are signaled to the brain. In other words, both the brain and the body are influenced by these commands, even though these commands are produced in a limited area of the brain, which reacts to a specific content of the mental process.

According to Damasio, the structures which form the proto-self are:

1. Numerous *nuclei of the encephalic trunk* which regulate body states and project the signals which arrive from the body into maps. Along these chains of signals, which start from the body and end in the brain, the encephalic trunk is the first region in which groups of nuclei signal the state of the body.
2. *Hypothalamus* and the *basal proencephalus* interconnected with the encephalic trunk areas. The hypothalamus contributes to the representation of body areas keeping an updated representation of the inner milieu: nourishing substances, glucose, concentrations of different ions, concentration of water, pH, concentration of hormones, and so on. The hypothalamus contributes in the regulation of the inner milieu according to these maps.
3. *The insular cortex, and the S-II and medial parietal cortexes* situated behind the splenius of the callous body, which are all part of the somato-sensitive cortices. The functions of these cortices, in human beings, are asymmetrical; they contain the most integrated representation of the inner state of the body and of the muscular-skeletal system.

- Localization of the nuclear-self

The study of patients with neurological damages shows that when nuclear consciousness is impaired extended consciousness is deactivated. But the opposite is not true, when the extended consciousness is impaired the nuclear consciousness can remain intact.

Nuclear consciousness arises from the interaction of the organism with objects. Objects are shown in the form of neural configurations, in the sensitive cortex specific to its nature. For example, in the case of visual objects, the neural configurations take form in a great number of places in the visual cortex.

According to Damasio, the nuclear self needs a high degree of structural stability in order to offer a continuous reference in the long period. This continuous reference is what the self is required to provide. Representations change in time, but the self does not change, or at least not to the same extent. This stability is an essential requirement for the creation of consciousness. It is therefore necessary to identity structures which are capable of producing this stability.

The enigma of the biological roots of the nuclear self was formulated by Damasio asking what is that thing which is unique, is it always the same thing and provides a skeleton to the mind? The answer which Damasio gives is that the stability is given by the borders of the organism. Life exists within borders, which separate the inner milieu from the outer environment. The concept of an organism is based on the idea of the existence of borders. In the case of a cell, the border is the membrane. Life changes continuously, but it can only change within certain limits: life needs borders. It is therefore necessary to study what keeps life within certain borders, together with the neural representations integrated with the inner milieu which describe the inner state of the living organism. Damasio states that without a body no mind can exist.

- Localization of the autobiographical self

Damasio states that structures of the second order, associated with the autobiographical self, need to:

1. Receive information through axonic signals coming from the sites involved in the representations of the proto-self.
2. Generate a neural configuration (image) which "describes", with some kind of time sequence, the changes in the maps of the first order.
3. Introduce, directly or indirectly, the general image which derives from the neural configuration of the flow of images. This general image is thought.
4. Send signals, directly or indirectly, to structures which process the information in such a way that the image of the object can be amplified.

This succession of representations constitutes a neural configuration which becomes, directly or indirectly, the base for an image, the image of the relation between the object and the proto-self modified by the object. The neural configuration of the second order arises in a transitory form from the interaction of some selected regions. It is not found only in one brain region, and neither everywhere or nowhere. The areas which meet the specifications for structures of the second order are the entire area of the cyngular cortex, the thalamus and some areas of the prefrontal cortex.

Neural configurations of the second order amplify the image of the object and this happens in different ways, it includes the thalamus-cortical modulation and the activation of the cholinergic nucleus and monoaminergic of the basal proencephalus and of the encephalic trunk, which all together influence the cortical elaborations.

These critical elements are set up by a network which is continuously reactivated and which is based on areas of convergence situated in the higher order temporal and frontal cortexes, and in subcortical nuclei such as the amygdala. The pace of this coordinated activity is set by the thalamus, while the prefrontal cortex, which participates in the work memory, maintains the reiteration of these components for long periods.

The list of the structures involved in the formation of consciousness is limited for the proto-self (such as those in the area of the encephalic trunk, the hypothalamus, the basal proencephalus and the sensitive cortices) and large for the extended consciousness.

- In conclusion

It is well known that vital functions, such as those of the heart, lungs and intestines, depend on the encephalic trunk, such as the control of sleep and wakefulness. Therefore, in a very small area, many structures are present which signal the chemical and neural states of the body to the central nervous system. These structures also carry signals from the brain to the body. Along these lines many centers control the vital functions of the organism.

An extended lesion of the encephalic trunk, which usually causes coma, compromises many structures which regulate sleep and centers which are associated to the proto-self. The brain nucleus which is dedicated to the regulation of life processes and to the representation of the organism share the same areas and are interconnected with the centers which regulate sleep and wakefulness, emotions and attention and, in a word, consciousness.

In conclusion, Damasio notes the essential role of the encephalic trunk: this region would be involved at the same time in the processes concerning sleep, emotions, feelings, attention and consciousness. This overlapping of functions could seem accidental, but according to Damasio it is reasonable when analyzed according to the model that he has developed. The homeostatic regulation which comprises emotions, requires periods of wakefulness (in order to collect energy), periods of sleep (presumably in order to reconstruct the chemical elements necessary for the neurons), attention (in order to interact with the environment) and consciousness (in order to provide highly planned actions). The anatomic link of these functions with the body is totally evident.

This description is compatible with the classical idea of a locus situated in the higher regions of the encephalic trunk capable of creating particular electrophysiological states in the thalamus and in the cortex. Damasio's description differs from the classical one in two ways: first, it offers a biological foundation to the origin and anatomical location of the proto-self; second, it presupposes that the activity of the proto-self offers an important contribution to the state of consciousness, but that it does not produce the subjective state which defines consciousness in itself.

Damasio suggests that mechanisms which produce consciousness have been selected during evolution because they are useful for the organism in order to survive. Because consciousness was necessary as a biological tool for survival it was not limited to emotions, but it was used by all the other sensory stimuli. At the end, consciousness became applicable to a wide range of sensory states.

Damasio underlines the role of the vagus nerve which enters the brain at a higher level of the encephalic trunk, well over the level in which lesions usually occur. A high number of signals does not propagate through the nervous system, but uses blood flow, which reaches the central nervous system at the level of the encephalic trunk. All the studies of patients with spinal lesions have shown that the higher the lesion the more severe is the impairment. The higher the lesion the less information flows from the body to the brain, blocking in this way the flow of consciousness.

1.2 Consciousness according to Edelman and Tononi

In this paragraph the model of consciousness suggested by Gerald Edelman and Giulio Tononi is briefly described. This model differs from Damasio's model because it introduces the concept of integration and amplification of neural signals and does not require a specific localization of consciousness.

Dealing with the scientific study of the neural basis of the conscious experience, Edelman and Tononi start their book "*A Universe of consciousness*" (2000) with a reference to what Arthur Schopenhauer (1813) defined as the "cosmic dilemma": "*how can the subjective experience be correlated to events which can be described in an objective way?*" According to these authors, the best way to solve this dilemma is the scientific approach in which theories which can be verified are combined with well devised experiments. Consciousness is not a topic of philosophy, but it can be studied using the scientific methodology.

In the last centuries, both philosophy and science have tried to explain the dilemma of consciousness. As far as the philosophical approach is concerned, Edelman states that it is quite improbable that philosophy alone will be able to solve the dilemma represented by consciousness and by the body-mind relation; at the most, it will contribute to define how difficult it is to deal with this dilemma. Thought alone, in the form of philosophy, is not sufficient by itself to unveil the origins of the conscious experience; it needs the support of observations and scientific experiments.

In the *"science of the mind"* a great progress has been made from the first introspective attempts of Tichener and Külpe. Now science can focus the attention on the neural correlates of consciousness, thanks to the technological advances of modern neurosciences. Nevertheless, Edelman and Tononi say that this does not allow to correlate the characteristics of consciousness with intrinsic properties of localized neurons in specific areas of the brain, as consciousness is not an object which can be localized in any part of the brain, but on the contrary a process. The aim of the authors is therefore to identify the neural processes which can explain the essential properties of the conscious experience.

Edelman describes this new perspective in the following way:

"Our analysis leads to several conclusions. First, conscious experience appears to be associated with neural activity that is distributed simultaneously across neuronal groups in many different regions of the brain. Consciousness is therefore not the prerogative of any one brain area; instead, its neural substrates are widely dispersed throughout the so-called thalamocortical system and associated regions. Second, to support conscious experience, a large number of groups of neurons must interact rapidly and reciprocally through the process called reentry. If these reentrant interactions are blocked, entire sectors of consciousness disappear, and consciousness itself may shrink or split. Finally, we show that the activity patterns of the groups of neurons that support conscious experience must be constantly changing and sufficiently differentiated from one another. If a large number of neurons in the brain start firing in the same way, reducing the diversity of the brain's neuronal repertoires, as is the case in deep sleep and epilepsy, consciousness disappears."

According to this approach, neural activities which are at the basis of consciousness involve large populations of neurons widely spread in the brain, and particularly the populations of the thalamocortical system. On the other hand no area in the brain is specifically responsible for the conscious experience.

In order to study the neural processes from which consciousness arises, it is necessary, according to Edelman and Tononi, to understand the global way in which the brain functions. For this purpose three main topological organizations of the brain, each one specialized in specific functions, seem to be necessary:

1. The thalamocortical systems, which constitute a group of separated but at the same time integrated circuits. This systems is based on the thalamus, which receives sensorial signals and signals of other nature and is connected to the cortex of the brain. Both the cortex and the thalamus are divided in many different functional areas. The different cortical areas and respectively the thalamus nuclei which are also specialized; for example, some areas process visual information and other auditive signals. These functional areas are separated by the reentry mechanism. The reentry mechanism is a key concept in the model suggested by Edelman. With the term "reentry" a process is characterized by feedback and feedforward signals. Reentry is a recursive exchange of information, and a parallel exchange of information among interconnected areas in which neural maps are constantly synchronized. The reentry mechanism, typical of the thalamocortical systems, turns perception into a unitary process and behavior. For this reason the mechanism of the thalamocortical systems seems to be dedicated to the integration of different brain areas into a unified response.

2. These parallel circuits, which link the cortex with the gland of the hippocampus, form a ring which project the information into the cortex through the thalamus. This organization differs from the thalamocortical system; connections are generally unidirectional and not bidirectional, and form long rings, and relatively few interactions exist at the horizontal level. These systems seem to be able to perform a variety of complex motility and cognitive procedures, which are generally functionally isolated among each other. This guarantees the speed and precision of the execution of different tasks.

3. Projections which start from the nuclei of the encephalus trunk and from the hypothalamus. These projections activate when major stimuli arise (strong noise, strong light, strong pain) and project information towards wide areas of the brain, releasing

neuromodulators which influence the activity and neural plasticity, and change the strength of the synapses in the neural circuits, producing adaptive responses. These systems are collectively referred to as systems of value because they signal to all the neural system the presence of a major event changing the synaptic strength.

Considering data which comes from neuroimaging studies, Edelman asserts that the neural processes of the conscious experience involve groups of neurons widely distributed (especially of the thalamocortical system) in quick and strong reentrant interactions. These interactions among multiple areas of the brain are necessary for a stimulus to be perceived in a conscious way. This assertion is supported by experiments conducted in conditions of binocular competition, in which a subject, undergoing measurements of brain activities with a MEG, looks at incongruent stimuli: red vertical lines with the left eye through a red lens, and blue horizontal lines with the right eye, through a blue lens. Even though stimuli are presented simultaneously, the subject will be aware alternately of one or the other. Even if both the stimuli are received at the same time, only one is transferred to the conscious experience. The results of these studies show that:

1. The brain areas which are correlated to the conscious experience are widely distributed, but locally specified.
2. The neural processes which support the conscious experience are highly coherent, in the way that the synchronization of distant cortical regions increases when the subject is conscious of the stimulus, compared to when he is not. Coherence is therefore an indicator of the degree of synchronization among areas of the brain, and the values of coherence can be used as the strength of the reentrant interactions among brain areas.

These results show that, in order to have conscious experiences, a quick integration of the activity of brain regions distributed through reentrant interactions is necessary. This aspect of the neural synchronization, even if necessary, it is not sufficient, by itself, for the emersion of consciousness. It seems that consciousness requires neural activities which are not only integrated, but also differentiated, that is to say a neural activity which changes continuously and which differs in time and space. In order to support this assertion Edelman shows that two phenomena which are characterized by the disappearance of consciousness are epilepsy and slow wave sleep. These phenomena are both characterized by the synchronization of neural populations where the majority of neural groups discharge in a synchronous way, with the consequent elimination of differences. Brain states become extremely homogeneous, and with the reduction of the repertory of brain states consciousness is lost.

In order to study the mechanisms underlying this integration of separated functional areas, Edleman studied the concept of reentry in a large scale simulation of the visual system in which no higher level structure coordinates the answers of the model. This simulation was created taking into account the functional separation of the visual cortex: the neural units inside each separate area of the model respond to different properties of the stimuli. For example, V1 group of neurons respond to the elementary characteristic of the object, such as the orientation of the borders in a specific position of the visual field; IT group of neurons (inferotemporal) respond to class of objects with a specific form, independently from their position in the visual field. This model was tried in different visual tasks, some of which required the integration of signals produced from the activity of multiple areas working separately. For example, one task required the discrimination of a red cross from a green cross and from a red square, all presented simultaneously in the visual field. These simulations have shown that the integration (which emerged very quickly, after 100-250 milliseconds from the presentation of the stimulus) did not occur in a specific area, but as an average coherent process, and as the result of the interaction of reentry interactions among groups of neurons distributed in many areas. Simulations have shown that reentry can solve the problem of the global and general synchronization. Reentry is therefore the key neural mechanism which allows to obtain the integration of the whole thalamocortical system; this integration can generate a unitary behavioral answer.

At this point, Edelman asks what integration is and how it can be measured. For this purpose he introduces the concept of "functional aggregates", which describe a subset of elements which interact strongly among themselves and in a weak way with the rest of the system, and which cannot be divided into independent components. In order to obtain a measure of the integration of a system, Edelman uses the concept of statistical entropy, a logarithmic function which reflects the number of possible ways that the system can assume, weighed according to their possibility of occurring. If the neural system is isolated (that is to say if it does not receive any signal from outside and inside) neural groups do not interact; any possible state of the system can occur, each one with the same probability. In this situation entropy is at the maximum and coincides with the sum of all the single entropies of each element. On the contrary, if in the system some sort of interaction is present, the number of possible states is inferior to what would be expected by the possible states which can occur when the parts are separated. This integration measures the reduction of entropy caused by the interaction of the elements of an integrated system.

Edelman and Tononi's are against any form of localization and this approach is well expressed in the dynamic nucleus hypothesis, according to which the activity of a group of neurons contributes directly to the conscious experience if it is part of a functional aggregate characterized by strong reciprocal interactions among a set of neural groups and in a time span in the order of a hundredth of milliseconds. Conscious experience requires functional aggregate to be very differentiated, as is shown by the high indexes of the neural complexity. The adjective "dynamic" refers to the fact that, even if a high integration is observed within nuclei, its composition changes constantly in time. The dynamic nucleus, generated largely, but not exclusively, from the thalamocortical system, is therefore a process, and it is defined according to the neural interactions and not by specific localizations.

In order to arrive at a general theory of consciousness and explain how the brain developed, Edelman suggests a theory based on Darwin's natural selection, known as Neural Darwinism, or the *Theory of Neuronal Group Selection* (TNGS). According to this theory, higher brain functions would be the result of a selection which occurred during the phylogenetic evolution of the specie, and the anatomical and functional variations since the birth of the organism. Since birth, brain is characterized by an excess of neurons and organizes itself according to a process which is very similar to Darwin's natural selection. According to the degree of utilization, some groups of neurons die, and others survive and are reinforced. Selection is operated not at the level of the single neuron, but at the level of groups of neurons, which can range from a few hundred to several million cells. TNGS, which describes the evolution of the central nervous system and accounts for its high variability (fundamental for the differentiation of the states of consciousness), is based on three principles:

1. *Selection during development*: during the development of the embryo neurons extend ramifications in many directions. Ramifications give place to variability in the connectivity providing an immense array of neural circuits. Some of these patterns will be reinforced according to their activities and neurons of these specific groups will connect more strongly.
2. *Selection with experience*: in addition to selection during development, a process of synaptic selection is the result of behavioral experience.
3. *Reentry*: reentry favors the synchronization of the activity of neural groups belonging to different brain maps, connecting them in circuits which emit signals. Reentry is the central mechanism which allows the space and temporal coordination of different sensory and motory events.

In conclusion, the neural Darwinism theory represents the example of a unifying research program, which goes from neurobiology to philosophy, even though there is not much empirical evidence which sustains it. At the moment it is criticized by the supporters of different theories and models.

The model suggested by Francisco Varela represents one of the most "global" models among those, in the field of neurosciences, which deal with the phenomena of consciousness.

Varela starts his study of consciousness in a paper published with Humberto Maturana entitled *"Autopoiesis and Cognition: The Realization of the Living."*

The term autopoiesis comes from Greek and means to "produce itself".

According to Varela and Maturana autopoiesis is the common element among all the living systems. An autopoietic system is, according to the authors, an independent unit capable of compensating, in a dynamic way, the perturbation which tends to destroy it. When these units interact and organize themselves in a greater autopoietic system, without losing their individual identities, different orders of autopoiesis are obtained, such as the transition from the cell to the neural system. Autopoiesis has to do with the question *"what is life?"* and tries to define life, beyond the individual differences of living organisms, using the common denominator, the so called minimal cell, which has in itself all that is common to living systems, discriminating in this way between life and non-life.

Autopoiesis is interested in the processes linked to life, in the belief that these processes can lead to the definition of what consciousness is. For Maturana and Varela, consciousness emerges from the characteristics of unity and autonomy of the cells: the living system tries to preserve its identity against all the fluctuations of the environment. Varela asserts that consciousness coincides with the identity of an autopoietic system.

In his last year of life Francisco Varela suggested a research program called neurophenomenology which has the purpose of unifying cybernetics, neuropsychology, theoretical biology, immunology, epistemology and mathematics in order to describe the phenomenology of consciousness.

In the paper *"From autopoiesis to neurophenomenology"* (Rudrauf, 2003) Varela suggests a general reference frame which unites all living systems: the concept of autonomy. According to Varela, the biological roots of individuality need to be located in the unitary nature, in the coherent unity of living systems from which autonomy derives. From the autonomy of living systems, and from their being a unity, identity takes form. Identity defies all the natural tendencies which try to destroy it, such as the law of entropy. The living system takes the form of a constant unity which is self-contained and which shows its identity and autonomy from the inside. According to Varela this unity is the result of processes of co-dependence among the different parts of the system.

Not to fall into vitalism, Varela underlines that his approach is totally mechanistic, as it is based on the principle of cybernetics and on the general theory of systems. Nevertheless, the model which he developed is different from that of Cartesian machines, based on input and output cycles. Living systems are characterized by the self-replication of themselves, while a machine is not capable of replicating itself. Varela asserts that the origin of life has to be found in the ability of self-reproduce typical of living systems; for this reason he considers autopoiesis the mechanism at the basis of life. According to Varela, the notion of autopoiesis is necessary and sufficient in order to define what life is. From autopoiesis an approach takes form centered on the system, on autonomy and self sufficiency of the organization. In this way, a transition from Cartesian machines and living systems, which are no more than machines with autonomy and unity, is performed. The finalized behavior which is observed in living systems is considered a distortion of the observer, which emerges when he tries to summarize the behavior of living systems. Varela emphasizes that cognition and behavior are mechanical processes and that life is not moved by final causes.

According to Varela, living systems are mechanical and their properties have to be found in the interactions among processes. In this perspective, what appears as intentional behavior is no more than the presence of specific mechanisms. Therefore also consciousness has to be considered as a consequence of mechanical processes. For example, an intentional act is a succession of mechanical actions which converge towards specific states, a transitory persistence in the relation between the living system and the environment. In Varela's vision persistence and stability are the elements from which consciousness takes form. In conclusion, mind develops from the interaction between the living system and the environment.

For Varela mind is not localized in the brain, but in all the organism, in the processes which link the living system with the environment. Considering that mind is generated by this interaction between the living system and the environment, it is impossible to say if it is inside or outside the body; for this reason, it is not possible to localize the mind. Varela suggests that the mind has the property of existing or not existing and that this depends on the processes and the interactions of the living system with the environment. Even if Varela expresses an immaterial vision of consciousness he continuously stresses the fact that consciousness and mind originate from mechanical processes, and that they are virtual mechanical entities. On the basis of this model, mind would be the consequence of the pattern of processes, which involve our physical body in interaction with the environment.

Consequently, an observer who studies the mind should put together the subjective experiences of the individual, gathered through subjective reports on the basis of different introspective methods for which he has been trained, with the description of how these physical processes propagate inside the living system in a dynamical way. Consciousness is for Varela the result of a dynamical and global process and should be studied as such. In this way he arrives at the conclusion that Chalmers' hard problem, the question about the relation between our subjective experience and the physical processes which can be observed in an objective way, requires the birth of a new experimental neuroscience of mind in which the subjective experience is integrated with the objective observation.

2

CONSCIOUSNESS
ACCORDING TO QUANTUM MECHANICS

In the 1930s, while the field of psychology was dominated by behaviorisms, which did not consider consciousness a field for scientific investigation, the most important interpretations of Quantum Mechanics were using consciousness in order to explain the strange behavior of the sub-atomic world. For example, according to the Copenhagen interpretation the wave function collapses into a particle only when a conscious observation is performed through an act of measurement. In this interpretations consciousness itself creates matter, and it is not matter which creates consciousness.

2.1 A short introduction to quantum mechanics

Quantum Mechanics (QM) or quantum physics originated at the beginning of the 20th Century in order to explain the behavior of the microscopic world at the atomic level. In this chapter Quantum Mechanics will be introduced shortly and some interpretations described, with particular attention to John Cramer's transactional interpretation in which the dual solution of energy is used and the concept of retrocausality introduced.

2.1.1 The double slit experiment: light as a wave

On 24 November 1803 Thomas Young presented, at the Royal Society of London, the double slit experiment demonstrating that light is a wave:

"The experiment I am about to relate (...) may be repeated with great ease, whenever the sun shines, and without any other apparatus than is at hand to everyone".

Young's experiment was very simple in design: a narrow ray of sunlight shines through a pinhole in a cardboard, the light then goes through two pinholes in a second cardboard, and then ends on a white flat surface creating patterns of lines, light and dark, which Young explained as a consequence of the interference among light waves. White lines (constructive interference) are shown when light waves add up, whereas dark lines (destructive interference) are shown when they do not add up.

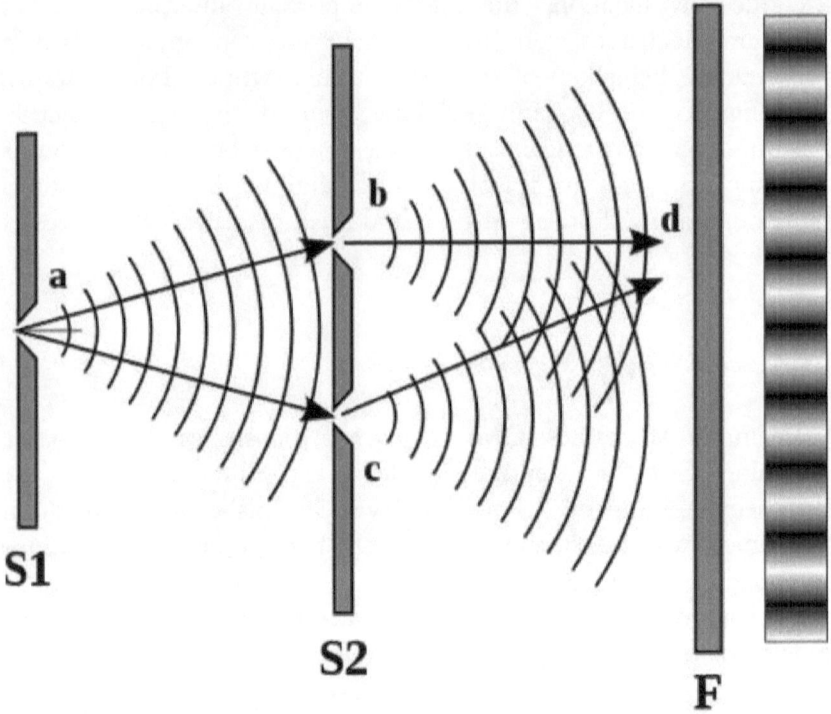

Thomas Young's double slit experiment

Young's experiment was generally accepted as the demonstration of the fact that light propagates as waves. If light would have been made of particles, the interference pattern would not have shown up, but only two well localized dots of light would have been observed in association with the pinholes in the cardboard. Instead, in the double slit experiment, the brightest line is located between the two pinholes, in what would have been expected to be a dark area.

28

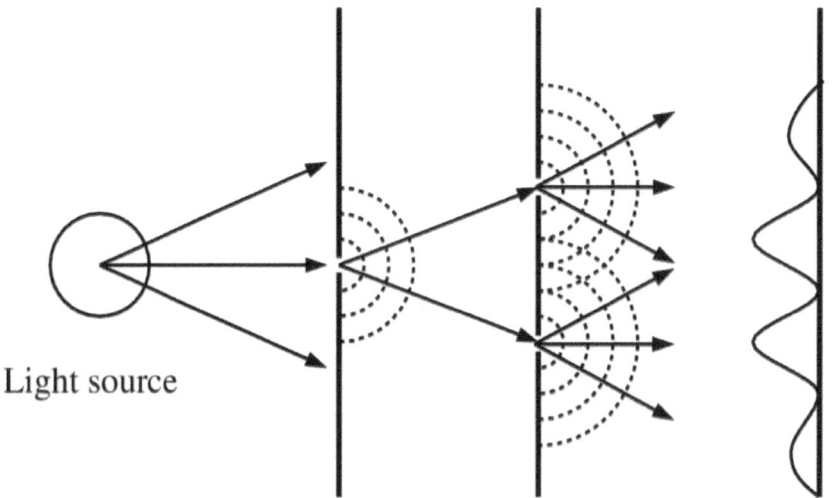

Light patterns in Young's experiment

Young's experiment has been considered the fundamental demonstration of the wave properties of light until Quantum Mechanics started to disclose the dual nature of matter: waves and particles at the same time.

2.1.2 The birth of Quantum Mechanics

At the end of the 18th Century Lord Rayleigh and Sir James Jeans tried to extend the equipartition theorem of classical statistical mechanics in order to describe thermal radiations.

In classical statistical mechanics, the equipartition theorem is a general formula that relates the temperature of a system with its average energies. The idea is that energy is shared equally among its various forms.

When applied to waves the equipartition theorem predicted that a body would emit radiations with infinite power, as it would all concentrate in the ultraviolet wavelength. This prediction was named the *"ultraviolet catastrophe"*, but fortunately it was not observed in nature. This paradox was solved on 14 December 1900 when Max

Planck presented a work, at the German Physical Society, according to which energy is quantized. Planck assumed that energy does not grow or diminish in a continuous way, but according to multiples of a basic quantum, which Planck defined as the frequency of the body (v) and a basic constant which is now known to be equal to $6,6262 \cdot 10^{-34}$ joule·seconds and which is now named Planck's constant.

Planck described thermal radiations as composed of packets (quantum), some small others larger according to the frequency of the body. Below the quantum level, thermal radiation disappeared, avoiding in this way the formation of infinite peaks of radiation and solving in this way the ultraviolet catastrophe paradox.

December 14, 1900, is now remembered as the starting date of quantum mechanics.

2.1.3 The photoelectric effect and light as particles: the photons

When light or electromagnetic radiation reach a metal, electrons are emitted, this is named the photoelectric effect. The electrons of the photoelectric effect can be measured, and these measurements show that:

1. until a specific threshold is reached the metal does not emit any electrons;
2. above the specific threshold electrons are emitted, and their energy remains constant;
3. the energy of the electrons increases only if the frequency of light is raised.

Classical light theory was not able to justify this behavior, for example:

1. Why does the intensity of light not increase the energy of the electron emitted by the metal?
2. Why does the frequency affect the energy of the electrons?
3. Why are electrons not emitted below a specific threshold?

In 1905 Einstein answered these questions using Planck's constant and suggested that light, previously considered an electromagnetic wave, could be described as quantum packets of energy, particles which are now called photons.

Einstein's interpretation of the photoelectric effect played a key role in the development of quantum mechanics, as it treated light as particles, instead of waves, opening the way to the duality wave/particles.

The experimental proof of Einstein's interpretation was given in 1915 by Robert Millikan who, ironically, had been trying, for 10 years, to prove that Einstein's interpretation was wrong. In his experiments Millikan discovered that all the alternative theories did not pass the experimental test, whereas only Einstein's interpretation was shown to be correct. Several years later Millikan commented:

"I spent ten years of my life testing that 1905 equation of Einstein and contrary to all my expectations I was compelled in 1915 to assert its unambiguous experimental verification in spite of it unreasonableness since it seemed to violate everything that we knew about the interference of light."

2.1.4 The double slit experiment and the dual nature of matter waves and particles

Young's experiment can now be performed using single electrons. Electrons used in a double slit experiment produce an interference pattern and therefore behave as waves, but at their arrival they give place to a point of light, behaving as particles. Do electrons travel as waves and arrive as particles?

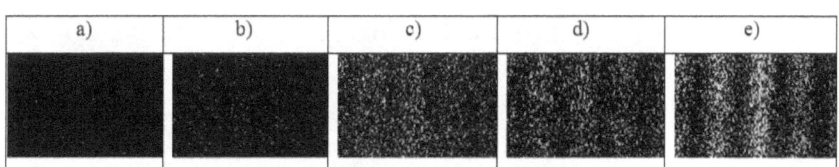

Double slit experiment using electrons
a) 10 electrons; b) 100 electrons; c) 3.000 electrons; d) 20.000; e) 70.000 electrons.

If electrons were particles we could conclude that they would go through one of the two slits, but the interference pattern shows that they behave as waves going through the two slits at the same time. Quantum entities seem to be capable of going through the two slits at the same time and know how to contribute to the interference pattern.

According to Richard Feynman:

"Double slit experiment is a phenomenon which is impossible, absolutely impossible, to explain in any classical way, and which has in it the heart of quantum mechanics. In reality, it contains the only mystery, the peculiarities of quantum mechanics."

2.1.5 Copenhagen Interpretation

The interpretation of Copenhagen was formulated by Niels Bohr and Werner Heisenberg in 1927 during a joint work in Copenhagen, and explains the double slit experiment in the following way:

1. Electrons leave the electronic cannon as particles;
2. They dissolve into waves of superposed probabilities, in a superposition of states;
3. The waves go through both slits and interfere creates a new state of superposition;
4. The observation screen, performing a measurement, forces the waves to collapse into particles, in a well-defined point of the screen;
5. Electrons start again to dissolve into waves, just after the measurement.

Essential components of the Copenhagen interpretation are:

1. The *Uncertainty principle* formulated by Heisenberg, according to which a quantum entity cannot have a precisely defined moment and place at the same time.
2. The *Complementarity principle* which states that a single quantum

mechanical entity can either behave as a particle or as a wave, but never simultaneously as both; that a stronger manifestation of the particle nature leads to a weaker manifestation of the wave nature and vice versa.

3. *Schrödinger's wave equation*, reinterpreted as the probability that the electron (or any other quantum mechanical entity) is found in a specific place.

4. The *superposition of states*, according to which all the waves are superposed together until a measurement is performed.

5. The *collapse of the wave function* which is caused by the observation and the act of measuring.

According to the interpretation of Copenhagen consciousness, through the exercise of observation, forces the wave function to collapse into a particle. This interpretation states that the existence of the electron in one of the two slits, independently from observation, does not have any real meaning. Electrons seem to exist only when they are observed. Reality is therefore created, at least in part, by the observer.

When Erwin Schrödinger discovered how his wave function had been reinterpreted into a probability function with mystical and ideological implications, he commented: *"I don't like it, and I am sorry I ever had anything to do with it."*

Einstein immediately refused the interpretation of Copenhagen stating that the use of the observer, of consciousness and probability proved the incompleteness of the interpretation.

According to Einstein a scientific theory had to use causality: *"God does not play dice with the universe!"*

2.1.6 EPR

In 1924 Pauli discovered that electrons have a spin, and that in a specific orbit only two electrons, with opposite spins, can find place (Pauli's exclusion principle). According to this principle any couple of electrons, which shared the same orbit, remain entangled showing opposite spins independently from their distance.

According to Einstein, causality is always local and information can only travel at speeds lower or equal to the speed of light, never faster.

Starting from these assumptions Einstein refused the idea that information relative to the spin of entangled electrons could travel faster than light. In 1934, he formulated these considerations in the EPR paradox (named after the initials of Einstein-Podolsky-Rosen) which remained unanswered for more than 50 years.

2.1.7 Aspect's experiment

EPR had been presented as a conceptual experiment, in order to demonstrate the absurdity of the interpretation of Copenhagen, raising a logical contradiction. No one expected that the EPR experiment could be really performed.

In 1952 David Bohm suggested to replace electrons with photons in the EPR experiment, and in 1964 John Bell showed that the change introduced by Bohm opened the way to the possibility of a real experiment. At that times even Bell did not believe that the experiment could be performed, but 20 years later several groups had developed the precision of measurements required and in 1982 Alain Aspect published the results of an experiment which showed that Einstein was wrong and that non-locality was real.

Aspect's experiment measured the polarization of photons. It is possible to force an atom to produce two entangled photons, which go in opposite directions. Each photon, of an entangled pair, have opposite polarization. The interpretation of Copenhagen predicts that when the measurement is performed on one photon it instantaneously determines the state of the second photon. This is what Einstein named *"a spooky action at a distance."*

Aspect measured the polarization of photons according to an angle which he could regulate.

According to non-locality changing the angle with which the polarization of a photon is measured would instantaneously change the measurement effected on the second entangled photon.

The experiment was conducted on series of entangled pairs of photons.

Bell's theorem stated that if locality is true, the measurements of polarization performed on the photons moving through the first apparatus, which could be regulated changing the angle, should always be higher than the measurements performed on the second set of entangled photons (*Bell's inequality theorem*).

Aspect obtained opposite results violating Bell's theorem and showing that non-locality is real. Einstein's good sense lost the competition against the unreasonableness of quantum mechanics.

Aspect's experiment, proved that in nature instantaneous correlations, where information propagates faster than the speed of light, are real and possible.

2.1.8 Wheeler's delayed choice experiment

When, in a double-slit experiment, a detector is used to measure which slit the photon goes through, the interference pattern disappears.

In 1978 John Archibald Wheeler proposed a variation of the double-slit experiment in which the detectors could be activated after the passage of the photon through the slits. In the delayed choice experiment the detector is located between the slits and the screen on which the interference pattern is observed. Quantum theory tells that when the detectors are turned on the interference pattern disappears, forcing the waves to collapse and the photons to go through the slits as particles. This should happen also if the detection is activated after the transition of the photons through the slits.

The delayed choice experiment became possible thanks to the speed of computers which can choose randomly when to activate the detectors between the double slit and the screen. The result is that this choice effects the way in which the photon has gone through the slit (wave/particle), and that this effect operates backwards in time.

The first two experiments which verified this model were performed independently in the 1980s in the University of Maryland and Munich, Germany. These experiments showed that the decision to activate the detectors affected the nature of photons backwards in time.

Wheeler, noted that it is possible to devise a double slit experiment at the cosmic level using light coming from quasars and a galaxy which operates as a gravitational lens on the way to Earth. This light would generate an interference pattern showing that light has travelled as waves. But if a measurement would be performed before the screen on which the interference pattern takes form, the pattern would dissolve and the photons would change from waves into particles. In other words our choice on how to measure the light coming from a quasar influences the nature of the light (particle/quasar) emitted 10 billion years ago. According to Wheeler this experiment would show that retrocausal effects operate at the quantum level.

2.1.9 *The transactional interpretation*

The transactional interpretation of quantum mechanics was presented in 1986 by John Cramer, physicist of the Washington State University.

In this interpretation the formalism of quantum mechanics remains the same, but the difference is how this formalism is interpreted.

Cramer was inspired by the absorber-emitter model developed by Wheeler and Feynman which used the dual solution of Maxwell's equation. As it is well known, also the generalization of Schrödinger's wave equation into a relativistic invariant equation (Klein-Gordon 1926 equation) has two solutions, one positive, which describes waves which propagate forward in time, and one negative, which describes waves which propagate backwards in time. This dual solution allows to explain in a simple way the dual nature of matter (particles and waves), non-locality, entanglement and all the other mysteries of quantum mechanics and permits to unite quantum mechanics with special relativity.

The transaction between retarded waves, coming from the past, and advanced waves, coming from the future, gives birth to a quantum entity with dual properties wave/particle. The wave property is a consequence of the interference between retarded and advanced waves, the particle property is a consequence of the point in space where the transaction takes place.

The transactional interpretation requires that waves can really travel backwards in time. This assertion is counterintuitive, as we are accustomed to the fact that causes precede effects. It is important to underline that the transactional interpretation takes into account special relativity, which describes time as a dimension of space, in a way which is totally different from our intuitive logic.

The interpretation of Copenhagen, instead, treats time in a classical Newtonian way, and this is why it required the introduction of consciousness, in a mystical way, as a means to solve the contradictions which it was encountering.

2.1.10 Other interpretations of Quantum Mechanics

Other interpretations of quantum mechanics, beside the Copenhagen Interpretation (CI) and the Transactional Interpretation (TI), are:

HVT (*Hidden Variable Theories*): it is based on the consideration that all the interpretations of Quantum Mechanics are incomplete, and that a deeper level of reality (a sort of sub-quantum world) which contains additional information on the nature of reality should exist.

This information is present in the form of hidden variables. If physicists would know the values of the hidden variables they would be able to predict in a precise way the results of specific measurements, and should not limit themselves to the "probability" of obtaining certain results.

De Broglie-Bohm GWI (*Guide Wave Interpretation*): in this interpretation, originally suggested by L. De Broglie and then improved and supported by D. Bohm, a wave which guides its movement is associated to each particle, like a radar which guides a boat. Mathematically this wave is described by the Schrödinger wave equation corrected by a factor which considers the guiding property of waves on the movement of particles. Differently from the Copenhagen Interpretation these guiding waves would be real and would permeate all the universe, guiding any particle.

MWI (*Many Worlds Interpretation*): suggested by Everett at the beginning of 1950, and supported by Wheeler, states that each time a choice is operated at the quantum level (for example if an electron can choose the slit in the double slit experiment), the universe divides in two and continues dividing according to all the choices which are operated.

2.2 Chronological order of Quantum models of Consciousness

In this chapter a short review of quantum models of consciousness is presented. Two criteria are offered in order to classify these models, and a choice is operated towards those models which allow scientific falsifiability.

2.2.1 Alfred Lotka 1925
Planck's constant and the objective and subjective consciousness -.

Lotka suggested his model before Heisenberg's uncertainty principle and the formulation of the interpretation of Copenhagen. Lotka's model can be considered the first quantum model of consciousness. Lotka suggested the existence of two types of consciousness. The first one, which he called deterministic, corresponds to the objectivity of the external world; the second one, which he called subjective, corresponds to the inner world (qualia). According to Lotka, consciousness of the first type (deterministic) is relative to all those phenomena which take place above Planck's constant. At this level it was considered that the deterministic laws of classical physics took place. Consciousness of the second type (subjective) would, on the contrary, take place below Planck's constant, where the deterministic laws of classical physics do not operate.

2.2.2 Niels Bohr 1930
Consciousness creates reality through the collapse of the wave function -.

The interpretation of Copenhagen proposed by Niels Bohr and Werner Heisenberg, suggests a direct link between consciousness and Quantum Mechanics. This interpretation attributes to consciousness an explicit role, through the act of measurement and observation, forcing the wave function to collapse into a particle and determining in this way reality itself. According to Bohr and Heisenberg consciousness would be an immanent property of reality which exists before the creation of reality.

2.2.3 Luigi Fantappiè 1941
Advanced waves and syntropy

Fantappiè starts from the d'Alembert operator which in Klein-Gordon's relativistic generalization of Schrödinger's wave equation has two wave solutions: *retarded waves* which diverge from the past to the future and *advanced waves* which diverge from the future to the past, and which for us, moving forward in time, correspond to converging waves, attractors/absorbers. Studying the mathematical properties of these waves Fantappiè discovered that the diverging waves are governed by the law of entropy, whereas the converging waves are governed by a symmetrical law, which concentrates energy, produces differentiation, structures and order, and which Fantappiè named syntropy. Fantappiè recognized the properties of the law of syntropy in the living systems, and concluded that living systems are a consequence of advanced waves. Starting from the mathematical properties of the laws of syntropy and entropy, the formulation of a model of consciousness based on the following elements is obtained:

1. *Free will*: which is generally considered a fundamental element of consciousness, is seen as the consequence of a permanent state of choice between information coming from the past and feelings coming from the future.
2. *Feeling of life*: another basic component of consciousness would be a manifestation of advanced waves, moving from the future to the past. When physical senses vanish, as in deep meditation, people experience states of consciousness in which past, present and future coexist. The coexistence of past, present and future would be a direct consequence of the coexistence of advanced and retarded waves.
3. *Non local memory*: Fantappiè suggests the existence of non-local correlations in the universe, as a consequence of the existence of advanced waves. For example, in living systems, memory could be a manifestation of non-local links with past events which according to Klein-Gordon's equation still exist.

Fantappiè's model is similar to the transactional interpretation of quantum mechanics and to the model of consciousness suggested by Chris King (1989).

2.2.4. James Culbertson 1963
Psycho-space.

According to Culberston memory, which is at the basis of consciousness, is a consequence of the change of state of matter in time. In other words, memory is equivalent to different states of matter in time. From this point of view memory is not formed by data stored in the brain, but by links between different states of space-time, and consciousness would therefore be located outside the brain, in the space-time. In order to describe this concept Culberston coined the term psycho-space. All objects of nature change their state in time. Therefore, according to Culberston, all objects of nature could be endowed with consciousness.

2.2.5 Herbert Fröhlich 1967
Bose-Einstein condensates

Bose-Einstein condensates are a state of matter which is reached at extremely low temperatures. These condensates show highly ordered structures which behave as one particle. Fröhlich found that during digestion the dipoles of cells align and oscillate in a perfectly coordinated manner. Fröhlich suggested that this behavior could lead to the formation of Bose-Einstein condensates at biological temperature. One important property of Bose-Einstein condensates is that they are able to amplify signals and code information; elements that according to Fröhlich are at the basis of consciousness. The work of Fröhlich inspired the model QBD (Quantum Brain Dynamics) of consciousness suggested by Umezawa and Ricciardi.

2.2.6 Umezawa and Ricciardi 1967
Quantum Field Theory (QFT)

Luigi Maria Ricciardi and Horoomi Umezawa suggested a model of consciousness based on Quantum Field Theory (QFT). This model starts from the work carried out by Fröhlich on Bose-Einstein condensates. The functions of the brain are seen as a consequence of collective quantum order states. For example, memory is associated to "vacuum states". In QFT vacuum states are the lowest level of energy in which, by definition, no particle is present. The stability of vacuum states make them ideal as a unit of memory. Umezawa and Ricciardi underline that one of the properties of vacuum states is that of developing correlations and order which can extend to the macroscopic level, producing fields which can affect the neural system. According to Umezawa, consciousness would be the result of the sum of quantum processes, while the neural systems would be limited to the transmission of macroscopic signals. The model of Umezawa was further developed by Giuseppe Vitiello.

2.2.7 Evan Walker 1970
Synaptic tunneling effect

In quantum mechanics the tunneling effect is a phenomena in which a particle violates the principles of classical mechanics by passing through a potential barrier higher than the kinetic energy of the particle. According to Walker, thanks to the tunneling effect electrons can pass from a neuron membrane creating virtual neural networks, parallel to the macroscopic network, and to which consciousness would be associated.

The macroscopic neural system operates through synaptic messages, while the virtual neural system would operate through quantum synaptic tunneling effects. The real neural system would follow the laws of classical physics, while the virtual neural system would follow the laws of quantum mechanics. Consciousness would be the product of the laws of quantum mechanics, even though the behavior of the brain can be described using classical physics.

2.2.8 Karl Pribram 1971
Holonomic model of mind

Karl Pribram suggested a holographic hypothesis of memory and mind. A hologram is a 3D photograph produced with the use of laser light. In order to produce a hologram, the object is first lit with a laser light, then a second laser light creates an interference pattern with the first one and the interference pattern is stored in the photographic film. When the film is developed only the interference pattern is revealed, but when this pattern is lit with a laser light, the original 3D object appears. When the holographic film is split in half and then lighted with a laser light, each part continues to contain the original 3D image. Even when the film is divided in minuscule fragments, each fragment will contain the original 3D image. Differently from classical photography, each part of a holographic film contains all the information.

According to Pribram, memory is not stored in a specific location of the brain, but works as a hologram. Only the interference among waves is stored. All information is transformed by the brain in a wave, and all the waves interfere giving place to holograms. According to Pribram, the same equations used to analyze holograms (Fourier transformations) are used by the brain to retrieve memory.

2.2.9 David Bohm 1980
Implicate and explicate order

Bohm introduced the concepts of implicate and explicate order. In the implicate order there is no difference between mind and matter, while in the explicate order mind and matter are separated. When we deal with quantum mechanics the implicate order prevails, while when we deal with classical physics, the macroscopic laws, the explicate order prevails. According to Bohm, consciousness coincides with the implicate order. In the implicate order particles are in-formed, take form, through the collapse of the wave function, and the implicate order coincides therefore with the process of in-formation, taking form. Bohm used the example of music in order to explain the implicate order. When we listen to a piece of music we perceive the implicate order, the information associated to the subjective experience of music, and not only the explicate order (physical parameters of sound waves, such as the frequency and amplitude). According to Bohm each material particle contains a rudimental form of consciousness. The process of information constitutes the bridge between mental and material properties of particles. At the lowest level of matter, the quantum mechanical level, the mental (conscious) and physical processes would coincide.

2.2.10 Nick Herbert 1987
Pervasive consciousness

According to Herbert consciousness is a property which pervades all nature, a basic force of the universe. Herbert reaches this conclusion analyzing the probability principle, the existence of matter (objects are formed only when they are observed) and interconnection (entanglement). These three principles are directly linked to the fundamental characteristics of consciousness: free will, ambiguity and interconnection.

2.2.11 John Carew Eccles 1989
Psychons

John Carew Eccles, received the Nobel Prize in physiology in 1963 for discovering that chemical transmission of neural signals in vesicles presynaptic reticules determines only one exocytosis. Exocytosis is the unitary fundamental activity of the cerebral cortex and seems to obey a law of conservation. With quantum mechanics it is possible to explain this law of conservation introducing specific particles, which Eccles named psychons. According to Eccles psychons would be units of consciousness, which would connect together in order to produce a unitary experience and experiments show that exocytosis is governed by quantum processes. Eccles believes that mind is a non-material field, analogous to a probability field and that consciousness is triggered by the exocytosis process.

2.2.12. Ian Marshall 1989
Quantum Self Theory

Marshall starts from Fröhlich's work and links the holistic properties of consciousness to the behavior of Bose-Einstein condensates. According to Marshall, conscious experiences arise when condensates are excited by electrical fields. Marshall believes that the collapse of the wave function always tends towards the formation of Bose-Einstein condensates and that a universal tendency towards the formation of life exists (anthropic principle). Mutations would not be casual, but would tend towards the formation of conscious life. The mental world (the conscious experience) would coincide with bosons (cohesive particles, such as gravitons and gluons which establish relations and can share the same states), while the material world would coincide with fermions (electrons, protons, neutrons) which do not share the same states.

2.2.13. Michael Lockwood 1989
Many Minds Interpretation

Lockwood refers explicitly to the Many Worlds Interpretation of quantum mechanics. According to Lockwood, feelings are intrinsic attributes of physical states of the brain and would all coexist together, giving place to as many minds as all the possible combinations of these intrinsic attributes. Consciousness would then select the feelings and the mind, but would not create them.

2.2.14 Roger Penrose and Stuart Hameroff 1989
ORCH-OR, Orchestrated Objective Reduction

Penrose starts from the assumption that reality is based on three worlds: the platonic world, physical and mental worlds. While in the Copenhagen interpretation the physical world is a consequence of the mental world (observation) through the collapse of the wave function, in Penrose's model these worlds are separate and interact together through the collapse of the wave function.

Hameroff and Penrose suggest that in microtubules, which are components of the cytoskeleton, every 25msec the collapse of the wave function takes place, producing a conscious experience which puts the mental world in relation with the physical world. The sum of these wave collapses would generate the flux of consciousness and an orchestration of organized states (Orch-OR)

2.2.15. Chris King 1989
Supercausality and consciousness

Chris King suggests a model based on the transactional interpretation of quantum mechanics (Cramer 1986) which starts from the dual solution of the relativistic wave equation (Klein-Gordon equation). King states that quantum entities are always faced with bifurcations between past and future causes which require choices to be performed. King refers to the works of Eccles, Penrose and Hameroff which show the relevance of quantum processes in living systems and suggests that according to the dual solution of the wave equation all living systems would be faced with bifurcations between causality and retrocausality. King names supercausality the sum of causality and retrocausality. These bifurcations would force living systems to operate choices which, according to King, are a common state to all living systems and to all the levels of organization of biological matter, from microstructures to macrostructures. As a consequence of the fact that all biological systems would act according to free will, and as a consequence of the fact that the outcome of free will is not determinable, biological systems always show chaotic dynamics which cannot be studied in a deterministic or computational way.

King suggests two levels of explanation of consciousness:

1. on the first level information moves from the mind to the brain as a consequence of the exercise of free will;
2. on the second level, information flows from the brain to the mind thanks to the amplification of signals performed by the chaotic dynamics of the brain, which usual take the form of fractals.

2.2.16 Matti Pitkänen 1990
TGD, Topological Geometro Dynamics

Pitkänen TGD model of consciousness is based on the hypothesis of quantum jumps which involve different moments of time (quantum jumps between quantum histories) and on the concept that everything is consciousness. According to this model the universe starts from an initial state of maximum consciousness which diminishes each time an interconnection (entanglement) is formed. In other words, consciousness would exist as long as it is not entangled, and consciousness can only be lost.

2.2.17 Alex Kaivarainen 1992
Hierarchical model of consciousness

Kaivarainen starts from the assumption that neural excitation depends on 4 waves:

1. thermal (de Broglie waves – B waves)
2. electromagnetic (IR waves)
3. acoustical (tr waves)
4. gravitational (lb waves).

For this purpose 4 new types of particles are introduced:

1. Effectons (waves tr and lb);
2. Convertons (interaction of tr and lb);
3. Transitons (tr and lb states);
4. Deformons (superposition of transitions and convertons).

According to Kaivarainen this model could justify condensates at biological temperatures.

2.2.18 Henry Stapp 1993
Quantum State Reduction and Conscious Acts

Stapp based his model on the assumption that consciousness creates reality (Copenhagen interpretation). Stapp developed Von Neumann's idea that the objective universe is a consequence of the subjective one, and concluded that only the subjective experience is real, and that we can only know our subjective perceptions. The Stapp model is based on three elements:

1. Reality is a consequence of finite events in the brain.
2. Each event produces an increase in consciousness.
3. Consciousness is the consequence of systems which observe.

2.2.19 Kunio Yasue 1995
Quantum Brain Dynamics

Yasue Kunio and Jibu Mari started their work from Umezawa's model and developed a model in which brain waves are described using Schrödinger's wave equation and the brain is treated as a macroscopic quantum system. Yasue suggests that consciousness arises from the interaction of electromagnetic fields and molecular fields of water in proteins. The evolution of the neural wave equation would not be random, but would tend to optimize the function of neurons. Yasue suggests a cybernetic model of consciousness which is based on the interaction among waves, and not on the physical neural network.

2.2.20 Giuseppe Vitiello 1995
Dissipative model of consciousness (QFT)

Vitiello developed a model based on QFT (Quantum Field Theory) which starts from Umezawa's works, in which "vacuum states" were considered as unities of memory. Vitiello underlines that a problem with Umezawa's model is that new information overwrites old information, losing old information. In order to overcome this limit Vitiello suggested a dissipative model of consciousness, in which living systems behave as dissipative systems in order to maintain inner temperatures compatible with the requirements of vacuum states (vacuum states require extremely low temperatures). When the brain is described as a dissipative system, it is necessary to introduce, in the mathematical formalism of QFT, the environment which absorbs the energy dissipated by the brain. In this mathematical formalism, the environment, in order to be able to absorb energy, must have a backwards in time direction, opposite to that of the brain. The cognitive function of the brain that Vitiello tries to explain is memory, which by definition is an irreversible process which moves from the past to the future. As a consequence the environment must move backwards in time, from the future to the past. Vitiello's model allows to increase the degrees of freedom and the size of information which can be stored in vacuum states, solving in this way the overwriting problem of Umezawa's model. Vitiello concludes that consciousness derives from the constant interaction of the brain with its double, which is the environment.

2.2.21 Massimo Bondi 1998
Synaptic junctions and consciousness

Bondi studied those situations during which consciousness vanishes, for example sleep, anesthesia and pathological conditions. These conditions (physiological, pharmacological and pathological), would demonstrate the global nature of consciousness which turns on and off when the neural structure (synaptic junctions) loses its computational property of quantum origin. The model suggested by Bondi is based on the existence of channels which spiral through the labyrinth structures of the cortical system creating a flux of particles which determine a constant state of consciousness.

2.2.22 Hupping Hu 2002
Spin mediated consciousness

Hu underlines that spin is becoming the key element of quantum mechanics. Hu associates each spin to a mental pixel. The model of consciousness which is derived has non-local and non-computational properties.

2.2.23 Flanagan 2003
Quantum theory and the foundations of perception

Flanagan suggests that the ultimate level of description of mind and brain ought to be the quantum level, insofar as quantum field processes mediate all chemical and biological processes. Flanagan explores a number of possibilities:

1. whether quantum fields constitute the ultimate level of description of biological systems;
2. whether this ultimate level is nested within higher levels of organization by way of the kinds of self-similarity found in neural structures;
3. whether this lowest level embodies the initial conditions upon which the brain exhibits sensitive dependence.

The thesis is that perceptual fields are coordinated with photon fields. Therefore the irreducibility of the secondary qualities flows from their elemental character and this might be in the form of:

1. internal state spaces of gauge theory;
2. additional spatial dimensions of string/M-theory;
3. hidden variables theory.

Flanagan argues that color vectors, considered as "immediately experienced qualities" together with their configurations in the visual field, ought to map to photonic vectors and their configurations in a photon field: vectors would get mapped to vectors, and fields to fields.

2.2.24 Alfredo Pereira 2003
The second order brain and the conscious mind

One way to avoid the Copenhagen/von Neumann metaphysics, while retaining a physical sense for the "collapse", is the concept of "decoherence". At first sight any isolated small microscopic system would be "coherent", in the sense that entanglement of particles/waves would be the rule, and any large macroscopic system would be "decoherent", in the sense that any property of this system, available to macroscopic observation and experimentation, would reveal no signal of entanglement between its elements. A widespread belief used to explain why nature behaves this way is the so-called "law of large numbers", that identifies the size of the system as the critical parameter for statistical cancellations to apply, thus generating a more probable behavior that would correspond almost exactly to the predictions made by classical physics. In this view, the existence of quantum coherence at the macroscopic level would be extremely improbable, and could not frequently and continuously occur in the conscious brain.

For the defenders of the quantum mind hypothesis, or even for physicists who have worked with quantum macroscopic effects, there must be something wrong with the "law of large numbers". Therefore, if the "law of large numbers" is not universal and/or is not really a physical law, a theoretical possibility opens, for a large macroscopic system such as the brain, to be continuously generating quantum coherent processes among particles/waves distributed in all its volume.

These processes would function as a "second-order brain", controlling and being controlled by classical processes that occur in that same system (the "first-order brain"). This "second-order brain" would be the ultimate support for the flux of experiences called "the conscious mind".

2.2.25 Timo Järvilehto 2004.
The organism-environment theory: consciousness and the Ultimate Essence of Matter

Järvilehto argues that the understanding of the ultimate essence of matter depends essentially on the conception of human consciousness. In the framework of the organism-environment theory consciousness developing with human co-operation and communication is the basis of any description of the world. Järvilehto claims that the properties of matter are relations created in human action/measurement. Therefore, there is no ultimate essence of matter, and the question "What exists?" is identical with the question "What can we know?"

According to the organism-environment theory the world that may be described appeared with the appearance of human consciousness. Consciousness was created in a system of several individuals when their actions were joined in the achievement of common results. This joining was possible through communication which later developed to language. As communication was needed primarily for the production of common results, language developed primarily for the description of the common results that were intended or achieved. This means words were not, in the first hand, used for the description of the world, but they rather act as indicators of common results. Therefore, language (and also personal consciousness mediated by the language) was primarily directed towards generation of the cooperative organization. Thus, a word is basically not a symbol representing something, but a proposal for common action. It is precisely the common result that is stored in language, and, therefore, the language reflects the history of mankind and its culture. Language is the historical collection of the results of human cooperation. Those parts of the universe which became objects of language were primarily those that were needed by human beings in their actions in relation to their bodies. Therefore, the perceived (conscious) structure of the world reflects more the structure of the human body, as it may fit the environment, than any independent structure of the world. The implicate order of the universe for man is the implicate order of the human body in its environment.

2.2.26 Baaquie and Martin 2005
Quantum Field Theory. The human Psyche as a superposed state

Baaquie and Martin consider the human psyche to be part of a universal phenomenon, and not specific and unique only to human beings.

Human psyche is described as a superposed state. In quantum mechanics, the spin of an electron has two forms of existence, namely the physical and the virtual. When it is observed it is in a physical state in which the spin points either up or down. On the other hand, if it is not being observed the spin is in a virtual state in which the spin can simultaneously exist in two mutually exclusive states. Every time the spin is observed, it is found to point in only one direction. Hence the virtual state can never be directly observed. Nevertheless only the human mind can see the virtual state. It follows that the human psyche itself must possess a similar virtual state.

In order to describe the human psyche two kinds of quantum fields are used:

1. one localized that refers to the specific individuality of the person;
2. the other which can overlap and include other's consciousness and requires a quantum superfield.

2.2.27 Donald Mender 2007
Eccentrically Subjective Reduction (ESR)

Donald Mender underlines that physicists today have two tools for comprehending the universe of observed physical phenomena:

1. the standard model of quantum field theory (QFT)
2. general relativistic gravitation, which lies outside the quantum domain.

Recent developments, including superstring theory, loop quantum gravity, twistor geometry, show that the behavior of gravitons, the vehicles of quantum gravity, has robust affinities with key properties of consciousness displayed only fragmentarily by either QFT or general relativity alone.

Roger Penrose and Stuart Hameroff postulate that, within the brain, physical "objects" constituted by gravitational field configurations mediate the self-induced collapse of linearly superposed, macroscopically diffused quantum wave functions into non computationally selected component states.

A post-objective science of consciousness, may require decentering the very plurality of physical observations themselves, beyond even the statistical influence of standard QFT. Specifically, the structure of quantum gravitational self-operators may change to include individual, independent acts of measurement.

The Penrose-Hameroff hypothesis might benefit from such a multi – subjective, decentered approach to measurement. The model would be enhanced and could be renamed Eccentrically Subjective Reduction (ESR).

2.2.28 Syamala Hari 2008
Zero Energy Tachyons and Eccles's Psychons

Although experiments to detect faster-than-light particles have not been successful so far, recently, there has been renewed interest in tachyon theories in various branches of physics. Hari suggests that tachyon theories may be applicable to brain physics. Eccles proposed an association between psychons and dendrons which are basic anatomical units of the neocortex for reception. Hari proposes that a zero-energy tachyon could act as a trigger for exocytosis, not merely at a single presynaptic terminal but at all selected terminals in the interacting dendron by momentarily transferring momentum to vesicles, thereby decreasing the effective barrier potential and increasing the probability of exocytosis at all boutons at the same time. This is consistent with the view of tachyons, which treats them as strictly non-local phenomenon produced and absorbed instantaneously and non-locally by detectors acting in a coherent and cooperative way.

2.3 Discussion

The quantum models of consciousness which have been described in this chapter can be divided in three main categories:

1. models which assume that consciousness creates reality and that consciousness is an immanent property of reality;
2. models which link consciousness to the probabilistic properties of quantum mechanics;
3. models which attribute consciousness to a principle of order of quantum mechanics.

Each model is associated to one of these three categories. Analyzing the quantum models of consciousness which belong to the first category a tendency towards mysticism can be observed. All these models start from the Copenhagen interpretation of quantum mechanics and assume that consciousness itself determines reality. These models try to describe the creation of reality as a consequence of panpsychism, and assume that consciousness is an immanent property which precedes the formation of reality. The concept of panpsychism is explicitly used by most of the authors of this category. These assumptions cannot be falsified or tested in an experiment.

1) Consciousness creates reality	2) Probability	3) Order principle
1930 - Bohr	1925 - Lotka	1941 - Fantappiè
1987 - Herbert	1963 - Culbertson	1967 - Umezawa Ricciardi
1989 - Penrose Hameroff	1970 - Walker	1968 - Fröhlich
1993 - Stapp	1980 - Bohm	1971 - Pribram
2004 - Järvilehto	1989 - Lockwood	1986 - Eccles
2007 - Mender	1990 - Pitkänen	1989 - Marshall
	1992 - Kaivarainen	1989 - King
	1998 - Bondi	1995 - Yasue
		1995 - Vitiello
		2003 - Flanagan
		2003 - Pereira
		2005 - Hu
		2005 - Baaquie and Martine
		2008 - Hari

Classification of quantum models of consciousness

Analyzing the quantum models of consciousness which belong to the second category, it is impossible to falsify the assumptions or test these models using experiments, as they consider consciousness to be linked to a realm, for example that of the Planck's constant, which cannot be observed by modern science.

Analyzing the third group of models which attribute consciousness to principles of order which have been already discovered and used for physical applications (laser, superconductors, etc.) it is possible to imagine experimental tests which could falsify them. It is though important to note that many of these models require conditions which are not compatible with the characteristics of biological systems. The order principles on which most of these models are based require extreme physical conditions such as, for example, absolute zero temperatures (-273 C°).

Using together the criteria of scientific falsification and the criteria of biological compatibility only the models suggested by Luigi Fantappiè and Chris King survive this selection. It is interesting to note that these models are not pure quantum mechanical models, as they both originate from the generalization of Schrödinger's wave equation (quantum mechanics) with special relativity.

2.4 Conclusion

In conclusion, it seems that all the models of consciousness which start from quantum mechanics cannot be translated into experiments, either because they cannot be falsified or because they are not compatible with the requirements of biology.

The only two models which offer the possibility to be translated into experiments are those which unite quantum mechanics with special relativity.

3

CONSCIOUSNESS ACCORDING TO
THE DUAL SOLUTION OF THE WAVE EQUATION

"Sometimes it is held that the key to the explanation of consciousness may lie in a new sort of physical theory. Perhaps, in arguing that consciousness is not entailed by the physics of our world, we have been tacitly assuming that the physics of our world is something like physics as we understand it today, consisting in an arrangement of particles and fields in the spatiotemporal manifold, undergoing complex processes of causation and evolution. An opponent might agree that nothing in this sort of physics entails the existence of consciousness, but argue that there might be a new kind of physical theory from which consciousness falls out as a consequence" (Chalmers 1996).

In the Copenhagen Interpretation of quantum mechanics, the collapse of the state vector (the collapse of a wave into a particle) occurs at the same time at all positions in space. This collapse would seem to require faster-than-light propagation of information, violating in this way the limit of the speed of light posed by special relativity in the propagation of causality. This was Einstein's original objection to quantum mechanics, which was later formulated into the Einstein/Podolsky/Rosen (EPR) paradox. Analyzing the EPR paradox, Schrödinger concluded that the problem lies in the way time is used in quantum mechanics. The Schrödinger wave equation, which was the focus of most of the discussion surrounding EPR, is not relativistically invariant and treats time in an essentially classical way. For example, it assumes that there can be a well-defined "before" and "after" in the collapse description.

The relativistically invariant version of the wave equation was formulated by Klein and Gordon in 1926.

In order to convert the Schrödinger wave equation into a relativistically invariant relation, Klein and Gordon had to use the energy/momentum/mass relation of special relativity:

$$E^2 = c^2p^2 + m^2c^4$$

where E is the total energy of an object, p the momentum, m the mass and c the speed of light

Combining Schrödinger's wave equation (quantum mechanics) with the energy/momentum/mass equation, the Klein-Gordon relativistically invariant equation is obtained:

$$E\Psi = \sqrt{p^2 + m^2}\Psi$$

The solution of the Klein and Gordon equation depends on a square root which always leads to two solutions: one positive in which waves propagate from the past to the future (causality), and one negative in which waves propagate backwards in time, from the future to the past (retrocausality). This dual solution is expressed in the form of: retarded waves (which propagate forward in time) and advanced waves (which propagate backwards in time). The Schrödinger wave equation has, in contrast, only the retarded wave solution.

In the 1930s the backward in time solution was rejected as it was considered impossible, even though experimental evidence supported this solution, as for example the neg-electron theorized by Dirac in 1928 and experimentally observed by Carl Anderson in 1932 and named positron.

Cramer's Transactional Interpretation (Cramer, 1986) and Costa de Beauregard's Advanced-Action Interpretation (Costa de Beauregard, 1953) show that the EPR paradox disappears when advanced waves are considered to be real physical entities.

3.1 Chris King's supercausality

Chris King starts his paper *"Chaos, Quantum-transactions and Consciousness"* (King, 2003) from Einstein's energy-momentum-mass equation, and states that all quantum objects are constantly faced with bifurcations which force the system to operate choices.

King suggests two separate levels of explanation of consciousness. In the first level, information flows from the mind to the brain, through free will; in the second level, information flows from the brain to the mind, thanks to the selection and amplification of signals performed by fractal structures. King considers the mind to be immaterial, and its organization a consequence of the cohesive properties of the backward in time energy solution (entanglement and non-locality).

King suggests that, in order to understand what consciousness really is, it is necessary to start from free will, because at this level it becomes necessary to definitely reject any attempt to use mechanical approaches.

King describes:

1. *Free will* as the process which the mind uses to act on the brain. Free will originates from bifurcations and supercausality which force living systems to operate choices. Retrocausality ($-E$) would be felt whereas causality ($+E$) would be perceived and processed rationally. In our daily life bifurcations would therefore be experienced in the form of the antagonism feelings/rationality. This constant antagonism forces humans into a state of free will and choice.
2. *Consciousness* is the aptitude of the brain to act on the mind, selecting and amplifying sensorial perceptions, thanks to the properties of chaotic dynamics and fractal structures.

Sir John Eccles underlined the importance of free will in the cognitive processes of people: all sane people are considered to have the ability to modify and control their own actions through will and intentionality. Free will is usually considered to be at the basis of all the actions of human beings, but it absolutely contradicts the assumption that only classical causality and determinism are real (Hooper and Teresi, 1986). For this reason, when starting the study of consciousness from free will, it becomes impossible to agree with the assumptions of deterministic models, such as the computational one, which describe the brain as a complex machine.

In this description, supercausality is the new paradigm which permits to overcome the limits of the traditional theories of consciousness.

The model of consciousness described hypothesizes that it should be possible to observe:

1. living structures at the quantum level;
2. fractal structures in the organization of the different levels of the brain, from the neuronal level to the main structures;
3. chaotic dynamics in the brain processes.

First hypothesis: quantum structures. The question about when a structure shifts from the laws of the microcosm (quantum physics) to the laws of the macrocosm is still discussed, but it seems that it is gradual at around 200 Angström (Arndt, 2005). In 1935 Eddington observed that synaptic vesicles had dimensions inferior to 200 Angström (Eddington, 1935) and, therefore, he hypothesized quantum-mechanic actions on living systems. These considerations were formulated again in 1970 by Eccles, who arrived at the conclusion that synaptic vesicles can be considered quantum objects, which can be therefore activated in non-determinist ways, following in this way the principle of free will which leads the system to global non-deterministic instabilities (Eccles, 1970). In 1987 Hameroff supported these considerations observing the fact that microtubules show dimensions which are inferior to 200 Angström, a fact which implies non-deterministic quantum processes. According to Hameroff microtubules are quantum objects (Hameroff, 1982).

Second hypothesis: fractal structures. The second hypothesis requires that the brain be organized on the basis of multi-fractal structures organized at different levels: the global level of the nervous system, the cellular level and that of the molecules. Fractal structure would allow the selection and amplification of signals, and the transition of the information from the lower to the higher levels, producing the *"butterfly effect"* which has been described by Lorenz in meteorology. In this way the instability of the highest neurodynamic level, could be influenced by the instability of the cellular level, which could be influenced by the instability of the molecules and of the quantum level. Empirical evidences show that the brain, neurons, cells and their components are fractal structures. A review can be found in the volume *"Fractals of brain, fractals of mind"* by Mac Cormac and Stamenov (1996). The fractal structure of living systems, and particularly of the brain, is now well known.

Third hypothesis: chaotic dynamics. Walter Freeman, worked for over thirty years studying the chaotic dynamics of the brain. In one of his books *"How brains make up their minds"* Freeman underlines the enormous complexity of the brain, and the inability of the linear causal model to describe and explain its complexity (Freeman, 2000). The brain is a highly dynamic and complex system: it contains approximately 10 billion neurons, connected in a complex non-continual network consisting of more than 1,000 billion synapses. According to Freeman, the functioning of such a network can be understood only by using models derived from the modern theory of non-linear dynamical systems, based on the properties of self-organization and emerging phenomena. Even simpler systems, such as the surface of a fluid or a mix of chemical products, which are characterized by a high number of interacting substances, can generate macroscopic and global properties under particular circumstances which do not exist at the level of the basic substances, and which are therefore indicated as *"emerging phenomena."*

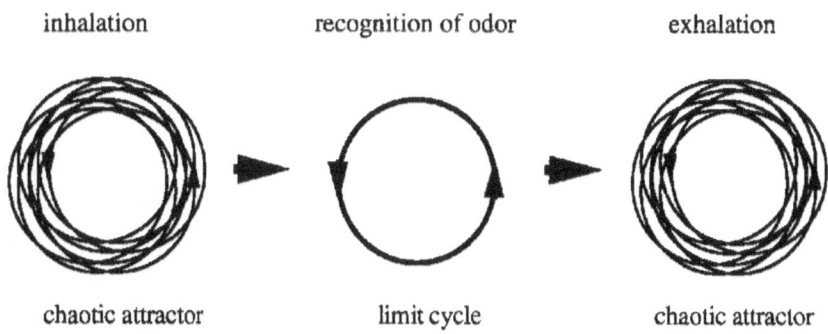

<table>
<tr><td>inhalation</td><td>recognition of odor</td><td>exhalation</td></tr>
<tr><td>chaotic attractor</td><td>limit cycle</td><td>chaotic attractor</td></tr>
</table>

Chaotic dynamics in the recognition of odors (Skarda and Freeman, 1987).

These properties depend upon patterns which result from non-linear interactions among elementary substances. From a physical point of view, these non-linear interactions can be traced back to feedback loops in which the components of a system are connected circularly in such a way that each element stimulates the following until the last one stimulates the first. Thanks to this circular organization, the behavior of each element is influenced by all the others. This permits the system to self-regulate until it reaches a dynamic equilibrium where the elements which are part of the system are affected by the global state generated together.

This circular interaction, or ring, permits the system to self-organize spontaneously without any external agent controlling the organization. In his studies of brain dynamics, using rabbits which were left free to smell the environment, Freeman found chaotic processes in the recognition of odors. Using EEG, Freeman measured neural activity during and after the odor stimuli, and represented them in space using a computational model. Freeman showed that the forms which were obtained, which were irregular but structured, represented chaotic attractors (or strange attractors, as described in the fifth chapter). Each attractor corresponded to the behavior shown by the system as a consequence of a particular stimulus, such as a well-known odor. In other words, a reaction to external simulation gives place to a global activity (registered by EEG) which is chaotic, but ordered and structured; if the stimulations change even slightly, the neurons instantly produce another configuration, which is complex but still ordered. According to the author, these chaotic dynamics can also be observed in other forms of perception.

In conclusion, Freeman says that:

"The great advantage that chaos can give to the brain is that chaotic systems can produce continually new types of activities. In our opinion these activities are essential to the development of groups of neurons different from those already established. More generally, the ability to create new types of activity may underlie the ability of the brain to reach for intuitions, and solve problems through trial and error."

Chaotic dynamics are defined as non-deterministic, and reactive (Schuster 1986, Stewart 1989). Reactive means that the system is capable of selecting and amplifying even the slightest perturbation, changing a chaotic system into a reactive system. At the same time a system of this kind cannot be predicted with computational techniques, because of free will which acts at each level of the system. The interaction of the chaotic and fractal properties repeated at the different levels (molecules, cells, neurons and nervous system) is indicated as the multi-fractal model. This model implies that all the components, from the molecular one to the global brain structures, can reciprocally activate each other. The fractal nature of their connections, the sophistication of neurons and synaptic junctions, leads to a modular and flexible structure.

According to King, the anticipatory properties of these systems, their flexibility and ability of performing decisions, justifies why this model has been selected during evolution. The advantage of conscious processes in terms of anticipation, flexibility, learning and self-organization are fundamental for the survival of the living system and therefore free will and consciousness have emerged, surpassing any eventual computational systems.

3.2 The model of Luigi Fantappiè

In July 1942 Luigi Fantappiè presented at the Pontificial Academy of Science the "*Principals of a unitary theory of the physical and biological world based on quantum mechanics and special relativity*" in which he showed that retarded waves (diverging waves), with causes placed in the past, governed chemical and physical phenomena which follow the law of entropy, while anticipated waves (converging waves), with causes placed in the future, correspond to a new category of phenomena governed by a law which is symmetrical to entropy and which Fantappiè named syntropy. Analyzing the mathematical properties of the anticipated waves Fantappiè arrived to the conclusion that these properties coincide with the qualities of living systems: finality, differentiation, order and organization.

The second principle of thermodynamics states that in each transformation of energy (for example when heat is transformed into work), a part of energy is dispersed in the environment. Entropy measures how much energy has been dissipated in the environment.

When energy is distributed in a uniform way (for example no variations in heat exist), a state of equilibrium is reached and it is impossible to transform energy into work. Entropy, therefore, measures how much a system is near to the state of equilibrium and which is the degree of disorder in the system. Entropic phenomena show the following characteristics:

1. *causality*: diverging waves cannot exist in the absence of causes which have generated them;
2. *tendency towards homogeneity*: entropic phenomena tend to level out in the sense that they evolve from differentiation to homogeneity, from complex to simple. With time homogeneity and the uniformity of the system grow: the entropy of the system grows.

The qualities of syntropic phenomena are the following:

1. Entropy diminishes.
2. Syntropic phenomena are anti-dissipative and attractive. Converging waves concentrate energy and matter in always smaller spaces.
3. Because the concentration of matter and energy cannot be indefinite, entropic phenomena should compensate the concentration of energy and matter. In syntropic phenomena an exchange of matter and energy with the environment is therefore expected.
4. Syntropic phenomena are generated by "final causes", attractors, which absorb converging waves. These "final causes" are strictly connected with the existence of the syntropic phenomena: in this way it is possible to introduce a concept of "scientific finalism", where finalism is equal to "final cause".

As a consequence of the fact that the universe is expanding, the macrocosm is governed by the law of entropy which forces time to flow from the past to the future (Eddington, 1927) and causes to precede effects (mechanical causation: cause-effect). On the contrary, in the microcosm expansive forces (entropy) and cohesive forces (syntropy) are balanced, and time and causes flow in both directions (cause-effect-cause), giving way to syntropic processes. Einstein's famous Übercausalität: supercausality.

The law of entropy implies that systems can evolve only towards disorder and destruction of all forms of organization; for this reason various biologists (Monod, 1974) have reached the conclusion that the properties of life cannot originate from the laws of the macrocosm, as these are governed by entropy and evolve towards heat death, disorder, and the annihilation of all forms of organization. Supercausality, and especially syntropy, which is observed in the microcosm, imply the qualities of order, organization, and growth which are typical of living systems.

Consequently Fantappiè suggests that life qualities are a consequence of the properties of the microcosm, of quantum physics. But, as soon as the syntropic system grows beyond the dimensions of the microcosm and enters the macrocosm it starts conflicting with the law of entropy, which tends to destroy any form of organization and structure. Thus the fight for survival, in the form of a conflict with the law of entropy, starts.

The conflict between life and entropy is well known and it has been discussed continuously by biologists and physicists. Schrödinger (Nobel prize 1933 for physics), answering the question about what allows life to contrast entropy, concluded that life feeds on "negative entropy" (Schrödinger, 1988); the same conclusion was reached by Albert Szent-Gyorgyi (Nobel prize 1937 for physiology and discoverer of vitamin C) when he used the term syntropy in order to describe the qualities of negative entropy as the main property of living systems (Szent-Gyorgyi 1977). Albert Szent-Gyorgyi states that *"it is impossible to explain the qualities, organization and order of living systems starting from the entropic laws of macrocosm"*. This is one of the paradoxes of modern biology: the properties of living systems oppose the laws which govern the macro level of reality.

The hypothesis of a fundamental conflict between life (syntropy) and the environment (entropy) leads to formulate a theory of vital needs.

For example living systems need to

1. acquire syntropy from the microcosm;
2. combat the dissipative and destructive effects of entropy.

In order to combat the dissipative effects of entropy, living systems need to acquire energy from the environment and protect themselves from the dissipative effects of entropy. These conditions are known as "material needs", and include:

1. In order to combat the dissipative effect of entropy:
   a. The need to acquire energy, for example with food;
   b. The need to reduce the dissipation of energy, for example with a shelter (housing) and clothes;
2. In order to combat the continuous production of waste, which is the consequence of the destruction of structures under the effect of entropy:
   a. The need for hygienic and sanitary standards and waste disposal.

The satisfaction of material needs leads to a state of well-being which is characterized by the absence of pain. The partial satisfaction, instead, leads to suffering in the form of hunger and illnesses. The total non-satisfaction leads to death.

Satisfying material needs does not stop entropy from destroying the structures of the living systems: cells die, and structures are destroyed; the living systems are therefore continuously called to repair the damages caused by entropy. In order to mend these damages syntropy is needed, as it is the only property which allows to create order and organization and to counterbalance the destructive effects of entropy.

Since the Autonomic Nervous System (ANS) supports the living functions of the organism it is possible to imagine that ANS needs to acquire syntropy from the microcosm.

Advanced waves (syntropy) concentrate energy, consequently:

a. when syntropy is acquired heat (concentration of energy) associated with well-being is felt in the thorax area (ANS);
b. when syntropy is not acquired void and emptiness associated with pain and suffering are felt in the thorax area.

When the need of syntropy is not met feelings of void and pain are experienced. When this need it totally dissatisfied the regenerative processes stop functioning, leading the system to death.

From this description originates the hypothesis that neurophysiological parameters of ANS should show behaviors of anticipation: pre-stimuli activations.

3.3 Pre-stimuli reactions

In the last decade a growing number of studies have shown the existence of pre-stimuli reactions in the parameters of skin conductance and heart rate. Anticipatory pre-stimuli reactions are neurophysiological responses activated before the stimulus takes place. These anticipatory reactions are activated before the subject can receive indications or cues about the stimulus. In scientific literature, various experiments show the existence of anticipatory effects, for example:

a. Anticipatory reaction of skin conductance. In 2003 Spottiswoode and May of the Cognitive Science Laboratory replicated Radin (1997) experiments which show an increase in skin conductance 2-3 seconds before emotional stimuli are presented. Spottiswoode and May replicated these results obtaining a statistical significance of p=0.0005, and performed controls in order to exclude all possible artifacts and alternative explanations. These results support the hypothesis that the autonomic nervous system reacts in advance of stimuli (Spottiswoode and May, 2003).
b. Electrophysiological responses. McCarty, Atkinson and Bradely in *"Electrophysiological Evidence of Intuition"* (2004) show the existence of strong anticipatory reactions of the

electrophysiological parameters of the heart.

c. Pre-stimuli heart rate differences. In his article *"Heart Rate Differences between Targets and Non-targets in Intuitive Tasks"*, Tressoldi and coll. report results of two experiments aimed at investigating pre-stimuli heart rate changes (Tressoldi 2005).

Scientific studies suggest a strong correlation among anticipation, feelings and neurophysiological measures of ANS in the form of skin conductance and heart rate frequencies.

3.3.1 Pre-stimuli heart rate responses: Tressoldi's experiments.

In the article *"Heart Rate Differences between Targets and Non-targets in Intuitive Tasks"*, Tressoldi (2005) describes two experiments, the first exploratory and the second confirmatory which show that the heart rate reacts in advance of the presentation of stimuli (p=0.015 in the first experiment, p=0.001 in the second experiment).

Experiment 1

The first experiment involved 12 subjects, 5 males and 7 females with an average age of 25.5 years (range between 24 and 45 years), mainly university students. These subjects were asked to participate in a computerized trial which was based on the ability of guessing. The participants were asked to sit on a comfortable chair in front of a computer monitor; on their left hand was applied a device connected to an apparatus which detected the heart rate. All the subjects had been previously informed of the progression of events, and that the sequence of the pictures which would be shown was random. Their task was to guess which picture would be selected by the computer as a target. Each trial consisted of 3 phases:

1. in the presentation phase 4 pictures (landscapes, animals, monuments) were shown for about 10 seconds, and heart rate data was collected;
2. in the choice phase the simultaneous presentation of all four pictures followed. At this point the subject had to guess the target picture.

3. As soon as the choice of the subject was made the computer performed its choice, using a random algorithm, and selected one of the four pictures and showed it on the monitor.

Data acquisition and the correct functioning of the heart rate measuring apparatus was monitored by a research assistant with his or her back to the participant. Owing to the automation of the target selection, the assistant could not suggest anything to the subject. The experiment ended after 20 trials.

The results of this first experiment show a statistically significant difference between the heart rate measured, during the presentation phase, in association with target and non-targets images:

a. *Target pictures* are those which are selected (using a random procedure) by the computer after the expression of the choice of the subject.
b. *Non-target* pictured are those which are not selected by the computer.

Before interpreting the results, the authors wanted to repeat the experiment on 12 other subjects, in order to exclude that the results of this first experiment could be a consequence of statistical artifacts.

Experiment 2

The second experiment involved 12 subjects, 5 males and 7 females, average age 25.3 (range 23-48 years). Also this second experiment, identical to the first one, shows a statistically significant difference in the heart rate when target and non-target pictures are chosen.

Discussion of the results

The results obtained in the second experiment confirm the heart rate differences between target and non-target pictures, which had been observed in the first experiment. The probability that the observed results could have been a consequence of statistical artifacts, even if always present, may be considered low because of the concordant findings of the exploratory and the confirmatory experiments, and the use of the bootstrap procedure which forms new groups of 12 subjects, combining 6 subjects from the first experiment with 6 subjects from the second experiment, and which has always produced statistically significant results.

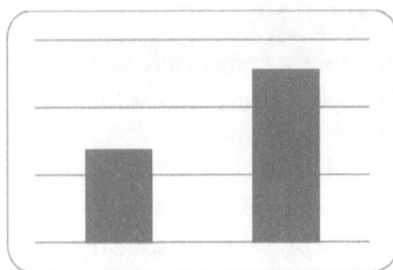

First experiment; p=0.015   *Second experiment; p=0.001*

Tressoldi concluded that with this simple procedure it has been possible to see a slight, but significant, anticipatory change in the heart rate, depending on the nature of stimuli (target or non-target), even though the choice performed by the subjects was totally random. In both the experiments, the number of guessed targets was equal to the quota expected by pure chance: 5 targets every 20 trials. Even though the sample is limited (altogether 24 subjects), 20 trials were carried out for each subject, enabling to underline even small differences between targets and non-targets.

Tressoldi refers to Damasio's model of decision making which is based on a dual system of information processing:

a. *Conscious system*, or declaratory, which uses verbal processes of reasoning in order to formulate decisions;
b. *Emotional system*, unconscious, non-declaratory, which uses a different neurophysiological network in which somatic markers, which can be measured through skin conductance and heart rate frequencies, seem to play a key role.

Tressoldi suggests the hypothesis that Somatic Markers (SM) can explain the pre-stimuli effects which are observed in these experiments and extends Damasio's model suggesting that somatic markers (emotional signals) can be the consequence not only of learning but also of the flow of information which moves backwards in time.

In a different presentation of the same experiments, Tressoldi and colleagues (Sartori, 2004) underlined that physiological reactions are still considered by most contemporary theories to take place only after stimulation has occurred. Yet recent studies have suggested that the autonomic nervous system can act as a reliable predictor of a future experience. Tressoldi's experiments show that the heart rate can anticipate stimuli giving support to the hypothesis that the autonomic nervous system anticipates stimuli.

Tressoldi recalls the studies performed by Damasio with somatic markers (SM) in gambling, and states that SM could be based on anticipatory effects.

In 1994 Damasio defined somatic markers (SM) as special instances of feelings which have been connected by learning to predicted future outcomes of certain scenarios. When a negative SM is juxtaposed to a particular future outcome, the combination functions as an alarm bell. When a positive SM is juxtaposed instead, it becomes a beacon of incentive.

3.3.2 Pre-stimuli skin-conductance increases

The Cognitive Science Laboratory (CSL) was established in the 1990s in California as an evolution of SRI (Stanford Research Institute) activities which had demonstrated the existence of quantum properties of the brain, and had been conducted under the direction of Harold Puthoff (quantum physicist) with the financial support of CIA and DIA (Defense Intelligence Agency). CSL research activity continues within the frame of US intelligence agencies but, differently from Puthoff's activities, the procedures are published and the experiments are therefore replicable.

The mission of CSL is to use the tools of modern behavioral, psychological, and physical sciences to:

a. determine which phenomena can be validated under strict laboratory conditions;
b. understand their mechanisms;
c. examine the degree to which they might contribute to practical applications.

In 1997 Radin observed anticipated responses of the autonomic nervous system 2-3 seconds before the presentation of emotional stimuli.

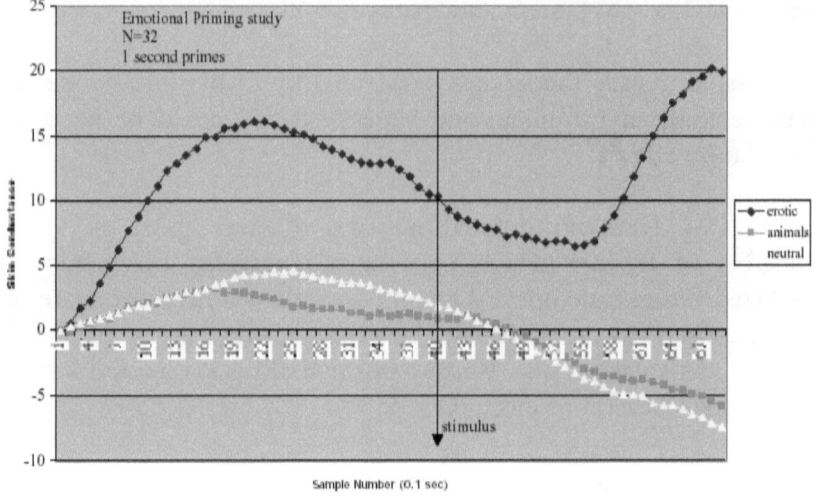

Average of skin conductance for 3 types of stimuli

Anticipation of events can play a fundamental role in intelligence activities. For this reason in 2003 May and Spottiswoode of CSL have replicated Radin's experiments with the aim of controlling all possible artifacts (cueing, expectation, stimulus generator, programming errors, data collection and computer anomalies, participant or experimenter fraud).

The experiment was modified in several ways, for example, instead of comparing erotic, neutral and animal images, the comparison of an acoustical stimulus generated by the computer with a "non-stimulus" (silence) was chosen. The subject used headphones which isolated from other sounds. The intervals between stimuli were variable, reducing in this way the arousal effect. All possible forms of cueing were controlled and eliminated.

The goal of this experiment was that of checking if the anticipated arousal of the autonomic nervous system (in the form of higher skin conductance) was significantly higher when neutral stimuli were used. The experiment involved 125 subjects who had never participated before in similar experiments. A Contact Precision Instruments device was used to detect the skin conductance, with an accuracy of ±0,1 µSiemens. The presentation of stimuli depended on an automatic generator, and subjects had no way of predicting the incoming stimulus. Stimuli were arranged in a continuous random loop and did not provide any sort of cue about the timing and type of stimulus. The intervals between stimuli could vary between 40 and 80 seconds and included the following sub-intervals: 5 seconds of recording of skin conductance before stimuli, 1 second during stimuli, 24 seconds after stimuli.

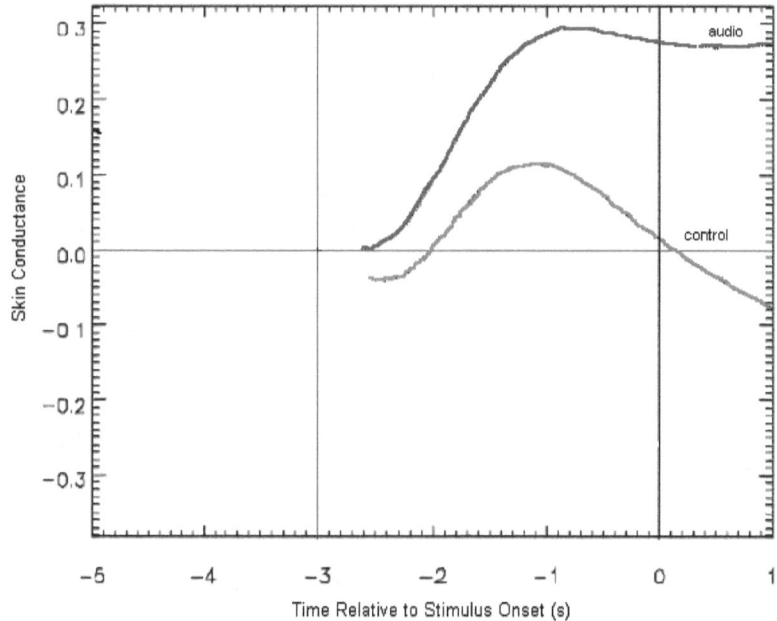

Pre-stimulus response of skin conductance; p=0,00054

73

Each session consisted of 20 trials (stimuli). As an average 10 stimuli were audio (identical 97-dB computer generated audio stimuli) and 10 stimuli were silent (control); the selection between audio and silent stimuli was performed after skin conductance was recorded in the 5 seconds period preceding the stimulus. Audio control stimuli (silence) were used to evaluate the arousal effect. Each session lasted approximately 25 minutes, at the end of which an audio message informed about the end of the experiment. Data analysis shows a statistically significant difference of skin conductance, between stimuli and non-stimuli (silence), 2-3 seconds before stimuli, reaching a probability level of p=0,00054. Skin arousal which anticipates control stimuli is markedly lower than pre-stimuli skin conductance and disappears while reaching the stimulus.

Mat and Spottiswoode performed controls for the following artifacts:

1. *Cueing.* Both the experimenter and the participant were blind to the upcoming stimulus type. The choice of the audio stimulus was determined by the computer using random procedures and after the pre-stimulus skin conductance was measured.
2. *Expectations.* The arousal effect was controlled using different pre-stimulus intervals, which were determined randomly by the computer.
3. *Independence of stimuli.* The correlation among stimuli resulted as equal to zero; the absence of correlations proves that it was impossible for the subjects to predict the nature of the next stimulus on the basis of the previous stimulus.
4. *Independent data analysis.* Data were simultaneously sent to the two experimenters who produced data analyses independently.
5. *Data gathering.* In order to check for artifacts the entire experiment was replicated using a skin conductance simulator, the behavior of which was known.
6. *Fraud.* Two different types of fraud were analyzed. In order to avoid the possibility that subjects could manipulate data, all data was stored in a binary 128 bit format which could not be read by commercial software. The computer was not linked to internet or accessible to subjects. The possibility of fraud by the

experimenter was controlled by independent data analysis; fraud would have required the agreement of both the experimenters. The replication of these results by other research institutes is the proof of the absence of this last type of fraud.

3.4 Conclusions

The empirical data which have been briefly described suggest a strong correlation among pre-stimuli reactions, emotions, and autonomic nervous systems (ANS).

1. Tressoldi's experiments produced evidence that heart rate frequency reacts in advance to stimuli. Tressoldi suggests that Damasio's somatic markers (SM) could explain these anticipated effects, and that anticipation could be the result of information moving backwards in time in the form of emotions.
2. CSL experiments replicated the results obtained by Radin, according to which skin conductance reacts before emotional stimuli are shown. These anticipatory effects are linked to the autonomic nervous system.

Tressoldi states that his research was inspired by the works of Bechara (1996, 1997), which show an anticipatory reaction of skin conductance in guessing tasks according to the positive or negative outcome of the choice, well before the subject can know the implicit rules which govern the game. Tressoldi also refers to Blanchard and Sharpe (Blanchard, 2000; Sharpe 1995) in which an anticipatory increase of the heart rate frequency is observed in gambling. In these works the authors conclude that the neurophysiological responses can convey information well before the subject can have any cue on the outcomes.

In agreement with the syntropic hypothesis of consciousness, these experiments indicate that the neurophysiological parameters of ANS show pre-stimuli reactions and that these reactions are mediated by feelings and emotions.

4

TIME AND CAUSALITY
SYMMETRY OF TIME AND SUPERCAUSALITY

King and Fantappiè's models of consciousness originate from the dual solution of the wave equation and from the concepts of time symmetry and supercausality. It is therefore useful to discuss in a more detailed way these concepts, comparing them with the concept of absolute time of classical physics.

The concept of causality is directly linked to the notion of time. For example, classical causation requires the perception, for us familiar, that time flows from the past to the future. Supercausality (causality and retrocausality), instead, requires the idea of unitary time in which past, present and future coexist and causes can move from the past and from the future.

Galileo and Newton can be considered the theoreticians of *mechanical causality*, on the basis of which all that we observe is determined by causes placed in the past. This type of causality is based on the description of a universe that moves from the past to the future: time follows an arrow in which the past can never come back, the future does not yet exist, and only the present moment is real. In this concept of time, the present is totally determined by the past.

Over the last century, the concept of time has been revised. The starting point was the famous *Lorentz transformations* which linked time and speed, from which Einstein's special relativity was born (1905). Einstein developed special relativity in order to extend the validity of Galileo's relativity to all the physical phenomena, in particular to the electromagnetic ones. Special relativity is based on the fact that the speed of light is constant. Among its major consequences the notions of space and time had to be redefined, and the equivalence between matter and energy. The idea of absolute time was abandoned, and time became relative to the speed of the system in which it was measured: this implies that two events which are contemporary in a particular speed system may not be contemporary in another, since time flows in different ways according to different systems of motion (Einstein, 1916).

4.1 Newton's universe and the life machine model

During the fifteenth and sixteenth centuries, the scientific revolution radically changed the concept of the universe which humanity had embraced during the Middle Ages, and opened the way to the understanding that we now have of the world.

The first signs of the scientific revolution can be traced back to the astronomical observations of Nicholaus Copernicus (1473-1543), which put the Sun at the center of the universe and showed the contradictions of the geocentric system, in which the Earth was placed at the center of the universe, based on the Aristotelian system. The Aristotelian system was introduced by Aristotle in the fourth century B.C., and perfected by Ptolemy in the second century A.D.. According to this system, the Earth is at the center of the universe and the Sun, Moon, Mercury, Venus, Jupiter and Saturn turn around it in circular orbits, each using a different sphere. These spheres were contained within a greater sphere of the fixed stars, behind which was the sphere of God. The new system proposed by Copernicus, which represented a huge innovation in the astronomical field, was heliocentric, placing the Sun at the center of the universe, around which the planets Mercury, Venus, Earth, Mars, Jupiter and Saturn all orbit, while the Moon orbits the Earth and the stars are considered to be still. Copernicus was followed by Johannes Kepler (1571-1630), who, thanks to astronomical tables, arrived at the formulation of the three laws of planetary motion, developing the Copernican heliocentric model into a scientific model.

The real change in the scientific approach, however, can be found in the works of Galileo Galilei (1564-1642) who, using the telescope which had just been invented, was able to empirically prove the hypothesis of Copernicus, and provide the evidence that the Aristotelian-Ptolemaic cosmology was not true. In this way, the hypothesis of Copernicus became the proven scientific model. The empirical approach of Galileo's work, and his use of mathematics, opened the way to the scientific revolution. The great contribution of Galileo can be found in the combination of scientific experiment and the use of mathematics. In order to use mathematics, Galileo studied fundamental properties which could be observed and measured.

In the same years, Francis Bacon (1561-1626) arrived at the formulation of the inductive method, deriving general conclusions from experimental results. He became one of the major assertors of the experimental method, courageously attacking the traditional schools of thought which were based on the Aristotelian deductive logic.

The Aristotelian method, starting from general laws, or postulates, deducts empirical consequences which have to be proved; Bacon's inductive method starts from empirical evidences to arrive at general laws. In order to produce objective knowledge, Galileo's and Bacon's scientific methods separated the observer from the observed.

This approach totally transformed the nature and purpose of science. Whereas previously the purpose of science had been to understand nature and life, science's purpose now involved the control and manipulation of nature. As Bacon said:

"Objective knowledge will give command over nature, medicine, mechanical forces, and all other aspects of the universe."

In this view, the aim of science became that of enslaving nature. A perspective which is far away from the concept of *"Mother Earth,"* which was totally lost when the organic idea of nature was replaced by the mechanical notion of the world, which can be traced back to the works of Newton and Descartes.

Descartes (1596-1650) based his work on the idea that the *"book of nature"* had been written in mathematical characters. His aim was to reduce all physical phenomena to exact mathematical equations. He believed that nature could be described using simple motion equations, in which only space, position, and moment were relevant.

"Give me position and movement," he said, *"and I will build the universe."*

Among Descartes' greatest contributions was his Analytical Method of Reasoning, according to which any problem can be decomposed into its parts, and then reordered. This method lies at the foundation of modern science, and has been of great importance, permitting the development of scientific theories and complex technological projects.

Descartes' vision is based on the duality between two reigns, separate and independent: the reign of spirit, or *res cogitans*, and the reign of matter, or *res extensa*. This division between matter and spirit has had profound consequences on culture, leading to the separation of body and mind which still puzzles science.

According to Descartes, matter and spirit are created by God, who is the creator of the exact order of nature that we see, thanks to the light of reasoning. However, in the following centuries the reference to God was omitted and reality was divided into the human sciences, linked to res cogitans and the natural sciences, which were an expression of res extensa.

Descartes' vision described the material world as a machine which has no intentionality and no spirituality; nature follows mechanical laws, and every aspect of the material world can be explained on the basis of its position and movement. This mechanical vision was extended by Descartes to living organisms, in the attempt to organize a complete natural science. Plants and animals were considered simply as machines, whereas human beings were *"inhabited"* by a rational soul (res cogitans) linked to the body (res extensa) through the pineal gland, at the center of the brain. The human body, on the other hand, was similar to the body of an animal-machine.

This highly mechanistic vision of nature was inspired by the high precision that was being achieved at the time by the technology and art of clock-making. Descartes compared animals to *"clocks with mechanisms and springs"* and extended this comparison to the human body, comparing a sick body to a badly build clock, and on the other hand, a healthy body to a well-constructed and perfectly functioning clock.

The scientific revolution reached its maturity in the works of Isaac Newton (1642-1728), who discovered the mathematical equations which govern mechanical motion, unifying the works of Copernicus, Kepler, Bacon, Galileo and Descartes.

Kepler derived the laws of planetary motion from the astronomical tables; Galileo discovered the laws of falling bodies; Newton combined these results in a general formulation of laws which govern the solar systems, the planets, and also stones (and apples).

He found that each body is attracted towards the Earth with the same force which attracts the planets to the Sun; he introduced the concepts of inertia and gravity, arriving at the famous laws which govern motion:

1. The *law of inertia* (already stated by Leonardo da Vinci and Galileo) which shows that bodies keep their movement until a force is applied to them.
2. The *law of proportionality between force and acceleration*, linking the force which is applied to a body with the mass and acceleration which is impressed, following the relation: $F=ma$.
3. The *law of action and reaction*, which shows that to each action there is a corresponding similar and opposite reaction.

The importance of these laws is their universality. They were soon found to be valid throughout the solar system, which was considered to prove the mechanical model which had been proposed by Descartes.

In 1686 Newton presented his complete concept of nature and the world in the *Philosophiae Naturalis Principia Mathematica* (Mathematical principles of the philosophy of nature). This work is a set of definitions, propositions and demonstrations that for more than two hundred years have been considered the most exhaustive description of nature and the world.

In the Principia Newton describes the experimental method which he adopted, which he derived from the combination of the empirical-inductive method described by Bacon and the rational-deductive method described by Descartes. Newton says that experimental results have to be resumed into theories, systematic interpretations, and deductions from theories have to be proved by experiments: in the absence of one of these two aspects, theories cannot be considered scientific. In this way Newton turned experimental methodology into the key element for the production of scientific theories and knowledge.

Newton's universe was the three-dimensional space of the classical Euclidean geometry: an empty space independent from what takes place in it. Time was considered absolute and not linked to the material world: time flowed relentlessly from the past to the future, through the present. In this space and absolute time, material particles, small solid and indivisible objects, were governed by mechanical laws. Newton considered these particles to be uniform, and explained the differences between types of matter as more or less thick aggregations of atoms.

In Newton's mechanics, all physical phenomena can be reduced to the movements of elementary particles caused by their reciprocal attraction: the force of gravity. The effect of gravity on a particle or on any material object is described by Newton's mathematical equations of motion, which are at the basis of mechanics. In this concept of the universe, empirical investigation could not extend to the elementary particles and the force of gravity: gravity and elementary particles were a creation of God, and could not be investigated.

In Opticks, Newton gave a clear description of how he believed God created the material world:

"I think that God first created matter in the form of solid particles, hard and compact, indivisible and mobile, made of such dimensions and shapes, and of such properties, to be the most adaptable to the purpose he had created them for; these particles are solid, harder than any other body, so hard that they can never be consumed or broken: no force can divide what God made at the moment of

creation."

In this way, Newton completed the vision of a gigantic cosmic machine, totally governed by mechanical laws of causality: everything originated from a precise cause, and could be determined using mathematical laws. Thus it would be possible to determine and calculate the future states of the universe, if the initial states were known.

During the seventeenth and eighteenth centuries this mechanical approach was used to explain even the smallest variations in the orbits of planets, satellites and comets, tides, and whatever was linked to gravity. The model was then extended beyond the boundaries of astronomy, and used to describe the behavior of solids, liquids, gases, heat and sound.

The mechanistic vision of reality is well summarized in the following words of Laplace:

"We need to consider the present state of the Universe as a consequence of its previous states and as the cause of its following states. An intelligence which, for a specific instant, could know all the forces which move the objects which constitute the Universe, and could analyze these data, would embrace in a single equation all the movements of the Universe and of the atoms: nothing would be undetermined for the future and the past." (Laplace 1795).

4.2 Thermodynamics and entropy: heat death

During the nineteenth century, the application of Newtonian mechanics to the description of heat lead to a new discipline: thermodynamics. This discipline, which can be traced back to the works of Boyle, Boltzmann, Clausius and Carnot, studies the behavior of energy, of which heat is a form. Gases at the base of thermal machines were studied and the transformation of energy into work was analyzed; this lead to the discovery of three new laws:

1. The *law of conservation of energy*, which states that energy cannot be created or destroyed, but only transformed.

2. The *law of entropy*, which states that when transforming energy (for example from heat to work) part is lost to the environment. Entropy is a measure of the quantity of energy which is lost to the environment. When energy lost to the environment is distributed in a uniform way (i.e. where no differences in heat exist), a state of equilibrium is reached and it is no longer possible to transform energy into work. Entropy measures how close a system is to this state of equilibrium.
3. The *law of disorder* which states that within an isolated system entropy cannot diminish. When an isolated system reaches the highest level of entropy no further transformation can take place: the system has reached a state of equilibrium, known as heat death.

The *law of entropy* is of great importance, as it introduces the idea of irreversible processes, such as that energy always moves from a state of high potential to a state of low potential, tending to a state of equilibrium. Sir Arthur Eddington introduced the expression "*the arrow of time,*" showing that entropy forces events to move in one particular direction: from a situation of high potentials to one of low potentials, from past to future. Our experience continually informs us about entropy variations, and about the irreversible process that leads to the dissipation of energy and heat death: we see our friends becoming old and die; we see a fire losing intensity and turning into cold ashes; we see the world increasing in entropy: pollution, depleted energy sources, desertification.

The term irreversibility refers to the fact that in physical processes there is a tendency to move from order to disorder, and it is impossible to restore the previous level of order in which all energy was available: mechanical energy dissipates in the form of heat and cannot be recaptured. If we mix together hot and cold water we get tepid water, but we will never see the two liquids separate spontaneously.

The third law of thermodynamics, derived from the second law, states that the dissipation of energy is an irreversible process, since dissipated energy cannot be recaptured and used again, and that the entropy of an isolated system (which cannot receive energy or information from outside) can only increase until a state of equilibrium is reached (heat death).

The term "entropy" was first used in the middle of the eighteenth century by Rudolf Clausius, who was searching for a mathematical equation to describe the increase of entropy.

Entropy is the combination of the Greek words "tropos", which means transformation or evolution, and the word "energy": it is a quantity which is used to measure the level of evolution of a physical system, but in the meantime it can be used to measure the "disorder" of a system. Entropy is always associated with an increasing level of disorder. In an isolated physical system, disorder (i.e. the homogeneous distribution of energy) increases leading to entropic heat death.

Nevertheless, this seems to be contradicted by life: living systems evolve towards order, towards higher forms of organization, diversification and complexity, and can keep away from heat death. Jacques Monod tried to explain life as the result of improbable conditions. In this way life could be considered compatible with the laws of entropy, but its survival was a continual fight against the laws of physics, which made life highly improbable.

Entropy evolves only in one direction: towards death and the elimination of any form of organization and structure. In order to become compatible with entropy, biology explains life as the consequence of highly improbable events constituted by the incidental formation of genetic codes and positive genetic variations. Entropy leads to the concept of a universe in which life is extraneous, a universe governed by laws which ignore life. Jacques Monod describes this, with the words:

"If he accepts this message in its full significance, man must at last wake out of his millenary dream and discover his total solitude, his fundamental isolation. He must realize that, like a gypsy, he lives on the boundary of an alien world; a world that is deaf to his music, and as indifferent to his hopes as it is to his suffering or his crimes."

In his work "*Dialoghi sui Massimi Sistemi*" Galileo provides a very clear description of his principle of relativity. He describes an observer closed in the cargo of a ship, who observes the way how objects fall. Galileo proves that it is impossible for this observer to calculate the speed of the ship basing his calculations on the way objects fall, because all these objects share the same movement of the ship (the same inertial system). Galileo points out that for an observer on the coast the movements of the objects on the ship would instead add to that of the ship.

For example, if a ship is moving at 20 km/h:

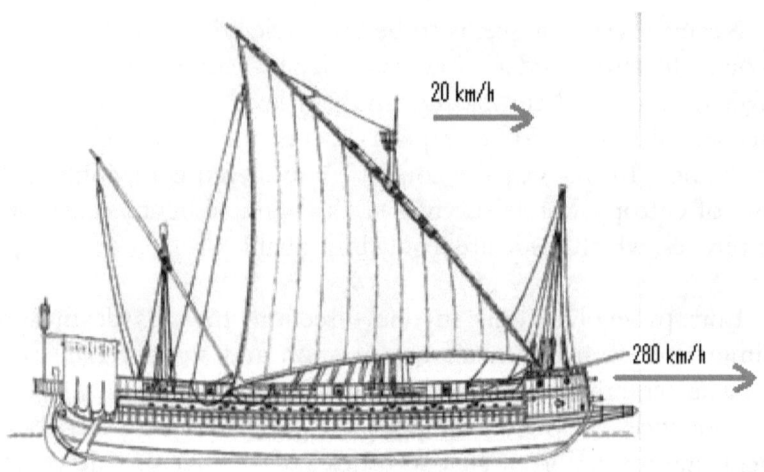

and a cannon ball is fired at 280 km/h in the direction of the ship, the observer on the coast will see the cannon ball move at 300 km/h, 280 km/h of the speed of the cannon ball plus 20 km/h of the speed of the boat. If the cannon ball were fired in the opposite direction to the movement of the ship the resulting speed would be 260 km/h, 280 km/h of the speed of the cannon ball minus 20 km/h of the speed of the boat (speeds are subtracted because they move in opposite directions). On the contrary for a sailor on the ship sharing the same movement of the ship (inertial system), the cannon ball would always move at 280 km/h in any direction he would fire it. Therefore, if an observer on the seashore sees the cannon ball moving at 300 km/h and the boat in the same direction at 20 km/h he can conclude that the ball was fired at 280 km/h.

Galileo's relativity is based on the principle that when changing an inertial system, speeds are added or subtracted on the basis of their relative speeds. In Galileo's relativity, speeds are relative to the inertial system, while time flows in an absolute way for all the systems.

Classical physics is based on Galileo's relativity.

4.4 Einstein's relativity and the coexistence of past, present and future

At the end of the eighteenth century Maxwell found that the speed of light did not add to the speed of the body which was emitting it, and Michelson and Morley proved experimentally that the speed of light is constant: it never adds to the speed of the body which is emitting it. Lorentz' profoundly innovative researches on electrodynamics and optics in moving bodies, lead to mathematical equations in which the speed of light is always constant.

In 1905, analyzing the results obtained by Michelson, Morley and Lorentz, Einstein found himself forced to invert Galileo's relativity according to which time is absolute and speed is relative; in order to describe the fact that the speed of light is constant, it was necessary to accept that time is relative.

As an example, let us imagine, after 500 years, an astronaut on a very fast space ship heading towards Earth at 20.000 km/s who shoots a laser light ray towards Earth (at 300,000 km/s). An observer on Earth will not see the laser light arrive at 320.000 km/s, as Galileo's relativity would predict, but will see it arrive at 300,000 km/s (because the speed of light is a constant). According to Galileo's relativity, the observer on Earth would expect that the astronaut on the space ship would see the light ray move at 280.000 km/s (300.000 km/s of the speed of light minus 20.000 km/s of the space ship) but, on the contrary, also the astronaut on the space ship sees the laser ray move at 300,000 km/s.

Einstein proved mathematically that what varies is time. When we move in the direction of light our time slows, and for us light continues to move at the same speed. This leads to the conclusion that approaching the speed of light time would slow down and stop, and if we could go at speeds higher than the speed of light, time would reverse.

In other words, events which happen in the direction in which we are moving become faster, because time slows down, but events which happen in the direction from which we are coming become slower, because time becomes faster.

In order to explain this situation, Einstein used the example of lightning which strikes a railway simultaneously in two different points, A and B, far away from each other (Einstein, 1916).

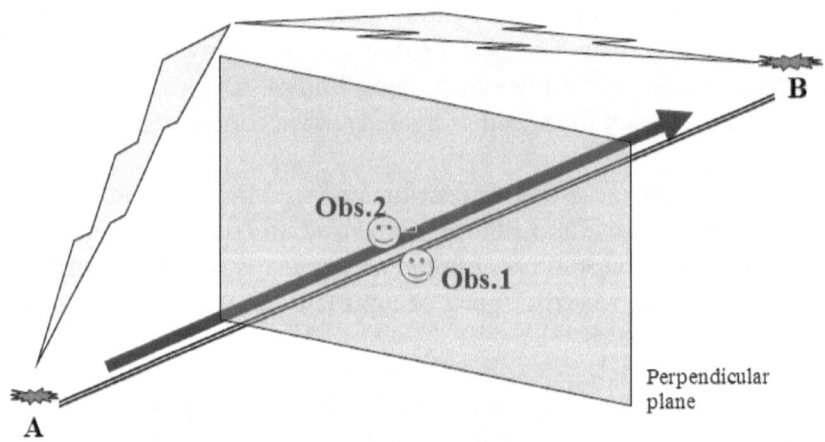

An observer sitting on a bench half-way would see the lightning strike the two points simultaneously, but a second observer on a very fast train moving from A to B passing next to the first observer at the moment in which the lightning strikes the two points would have already experienced the lightning striking point B, but would have not experienced the lightning striking point A. Even if the two observers share the same point of space at the same moment, they cannot agree on the events which are happening in the direction in which the second observer is moving. Agreeing on the existence of contemporary events is therefore linked to the speed at which the observers are moving.

In other words, events which take place in the direction in which we are moving become faster, because our time slows down; but events which happen in the direction opposite to our movement become slower, because our time speeds up.

It is important to note that time flows differently if the event is happening in the direction towards which we are moving, or in the direction from which we are coming: in the first case they become slower and in the second case faster.

This example is limited to two observers; but what happens when we compare more than two observers moving in different directions at high speeds?

The first couple (one on the bench and the other in the train) can reach an agreement only on the contemporary existence of events which happen on a plane perpendicular to the movement of the train. If we add a third observer moving in another direction, but sharing the same place and moment with the other two observers, they would agree only on events placed on a line which unites the two perpendicular planes; if we add a fourth observer, they would agree only on a point which unites the three perpendicular planes; if we add a fifth observer, who is not even sharing the same point in space, no agreement would be possible at all.

If we consider that only what happens in the same moment exists (Newton's time concept), we would be forced to conclude that reality does not exist. In order to re-establish an agreement between the different observers, and in this way the existence of reality, we need to accept the coexistence of events which could be future or past for us, but contemporary for another observer. Extending these considerations, we arrive at the necessary consequence that past, present and future coexist.

Einstein himself found it difficult to accept this consequence of special relativity, according to which past, present and future coexist; but the unified time model was perfected by Minkowski, who coined the term *chronotope* to describe the union of space and time.

Since Einstein presented his theory of relativity, time has become a dimension of space: space is no longer limited to 3 dimensions. As we can move in space, so we can also move in time: space now has 4 dimensions, and is therefore named space-time.

Another important consequence of the theory of relativity is that mass is a form of energy, and even a stationary object has energy in its mass. The relation between mass and energy is expressed by the famous equation $E=mc^2$, where c is the speed of light, m the mass and e the energy. The equivalence between mass and energy opened the way to quantum mechanics, where mass is no longer associated with a material substance, but seen as a type of energy. Particles are therefore now studied according to relativity, where time and space are united in a four-dimensional continuum. Atomic particles are now considered dynamically to be forms of time-space: their space form makes them appear as objects with mass, while their time form makes them appear as waves with energy. Since the introduction of relativity, matter and its activity are two aspects which can no longer be separated: they are two forms of the same space-time unity.

4.5 Symmetry of time, supercausality and retrocausality

Changes of paradigm often coincided with counterintuitive discoveries:

1. It was intuitive to imagine Earth to be flat, but counterintuitive to imagine it round;
2. It was intuitive to imagine the Sun orbiting around the Earth, but counterintuitive to imagine the Earth orbiting around the Sun.

Nowadays it is intuitive to imagine time which flows from the past to the future, but counterintuitive to imagine that past, present and future coexist!

Einstein's relativity started a new description of reality which is symmetrical in respect of time: on one side energy and waves which propagate from the past to the future, on the other side energy and waves which propagate backwards in time from the future to the past, and which we experiment as attractors.

Einstein used the term *Übercausalität* (supercausality) to refer to this new model of causality.

The equation $E=mc^2$, commonly associated with the work of Albert Einstein, was first published in 1890 by Oliver Heaviside and then refined by Henri Poincaré in 1900 and Olinto De Pretto in 1903, and it then become famous with Einstein's special relativity where it was integrated with the momentum in the energy/momentum/mass equation:

$$E^2 = p^2c^2 + m^2c^4$$
which relates energy (E), momentum (p) and mass (m)

In order to calculate the value of energy it is necessary to operate a square root which produces always two solutions, one positive and one negative. This simple property of square roots implies that the solution of energy is always dual: positive ($+E$) and negative ($-E$).

According to Einstein's special relativity:

1. the positive energy solution ($+E$) describes energy which diverges from causes located in the past and which propagates towards the future (*retarded potentials*);
2. the negative energy solution ($-E$) describes energy which diverges from causes located in the future and which propagates backwards in time from the future towards the past (*advanced potentials*).

The negative energy solution was immediately considered impossible, a mathematical trick, because it implied the existence of causes located in the future which retroacted on the past. This absurd situation was automatically solved in inertial systems in which the momentum (p) is equal to zero. When the momentum equals to zero $c^2p^2=0$ and the equation simplifies in the famous $E = mc^2$ which has only positive solutions ($+E$).

But, in 1924, Wolfgang Pauli (Nobel prize 1945) discovered the spin of the electrons. The spin consists of a momentum (p) which can never be equal to zero: even an object which is totally still has momentum derived from the spin of electrons which form it. As a consequence of the energy associated to the spin, the energy/momentum/mass equation could no longer be simplified in the $E = mc^2$.

In 1926 Klein and Gordon generalized Schrödinger's wave equation (Ψ) into a relativistic invariant equation by inserting the energy/momentum/mass equation. In this way, Klein and Gordon discovered the existence of a dual wave solution: retarded waves which propagate from the past to the future ($+E\Psi$) and advanced waves which propagate from the future to the past ($-E\Psi$).

In 1928 Paul Dirac tried to solve the unacceptable negative solution by applying the energy/momentum/mass equation to the study of electrons, turning them into relativistic objects. But, also in this case, the unwanted negative solution emerged in the form of electrons (e-) and its antiparticles ($e+$).

The antiparticle of the electron, initially named neg-electron, was experimentally observed in 1932 by Carl Anderson in cosmic rays and named positron. Anderson become the first person who proved empirically the existence of the negative energy solution and of waves which propagate backwards from the future to the past: the negative solution was no longer an impossible mathematical absurdity, but it became empirical evidence. Dirac's equation predicts a universe made of matter which moves forward in time and antimatter which moves backwards in time.

In his book "*The Road to Reality*" Roger Penrose underlines that usually physicists tend to reject as "unphysical" any solution which contradicts classical causality, according to which causes always precede effects. Any solution which makes it possible to send a signal backwards in time is usually rejected.

Even if Penrose chose to reject the negative solution of the energy equation, he states that this refusal is a consequence of a subjective choice, towards which other physicists have different opinions.

Penrose dedicates nearly 200 pages of his book to the paradox of the negative solution. According to Penrose it is important that the value of E is always positive because negative values of E lead to catastrophic instabilities in the Standard Model of sub-atomic physics.

"Unfortunately in relativistic particles both solutions of the equation need to be considered as a possibility, even a nonphysical negative energy has to be considered as a possibility. This does not happen in non-relativistic particles. In this last case, the quantity is always defined as positive, and the embarrassing negative solution does not appear."

Penrose adds that the relativistic version of Schrödinger's equation does not offer a procedure in order to exclude the negative solution. In the case of a single particle this does not lead to any real problem, however when particles interact, the wave function cannot yield only the positive solution. This creates a conflict with the law of classical causation.

In order to remove the embarrassing negative solution, Dirac suggested in 1931 an hypothesis which Penrose describes simply as crazy. Dirac used Pauli's principle, according to which two electrons cannot share the same state, to suggest that all states of negative energy are occupied, thereby forbidding any interaction between positive and negative states of matter. This ocean of negative energy which occupies all positive states is called Dirac sea.

The Standard Model of physics is based on this assumption.

Even if classical physics rejects the negative solution of energy and the possibility of retrocausality, several respected scientists have worked and are working on this possibility.

An example are Feynman's diagrams of electron-positron annihilation, according to which electrons are not destroyed by the contact with positrons, but the release of energy is caused by electrons changing direction in time and becoming positrons.

When Feynman's diagrams are interpreted they imply necessarily the existence of retrocausality (Feynman, 1949). Feynman has also used the concept of retrocausality to produce a model of positrons which reinterprets Dirac's hypothesis on the sea of negative energy occupying all possible states. In this model, electrons which move backwards in time would acquire positive charges (Wheeler 1945).

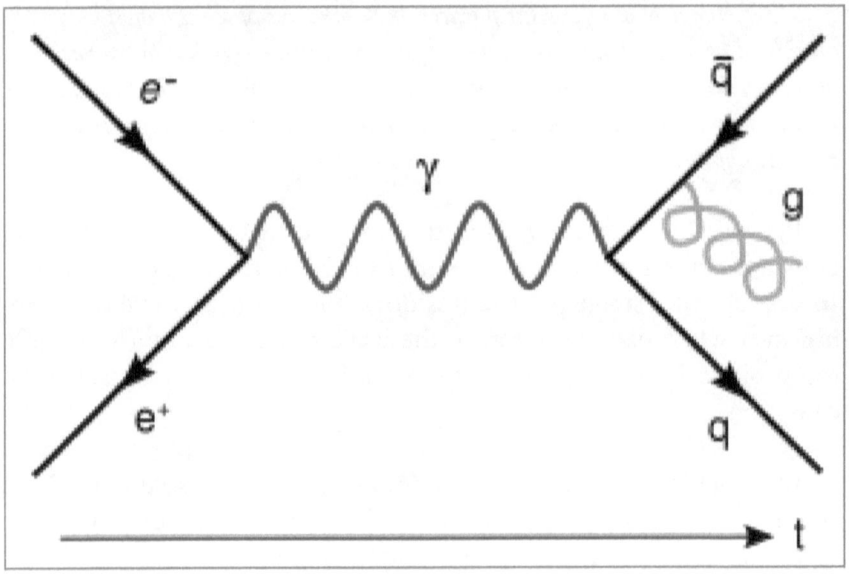

Yoichiro Nambu has applied Feynman's model to the processes of annihilation of particle-antiparticle couples, arriving at the conclusion that it is not a process of annihilation or creation of couples of particles and antiparticles, but simply a change of the time direction of particles, from the past to the future or from the future to the past (Nambu 1950).

Costa de Beauregard used the concept of retrocausality in order to explain entanglement (de Beauregard, 1977) and in 1986 John Cramer, physicist at the Washington State University, formulated his transaction interpretation, inspired by the absorber-emitter model developed by Wheeler and Feynman. Cramer notes that the generalization of Schrödinger's wave equation into a relativistic invariant equation (Klein-Gordon 1926) has two solutions, one positive, which describes waves which propagate forward in time, and one negative, which describes waves which propagate backwards in time. This dual solution would explain the dual nature of matter (particles and waves), non-locality and all the other mysteries of quantum mechanics leaving the formalism of quantum mechanics the same.

Until the XIX century, time was considered to be irreversible, a sequence of absolute moments. In 1954 the philosopher Michael Dummet showed that there is no philosophical contradiction in the idea that effects can precede causes (Dummet, 1954).

Fantappiè added to this discussion a new element. He showed that diverging waves, in which causes are located in the past, are governed by the *law of entropy*; while converging waves, in which causes are located in the future, are governed by the *law of syntropy*.

5

METHODOLOGY

In order to test the existence of retrocausal effects, the fundamental condition is the availability of unpredictable sequences, that is to say pure random sequences.

This chapter:

1. Starts with a short description of the properties of random sequences and of the difference between random and pseudorandom sequences, and the methodology used in order to obtain pure random sequences using common PCs.

2. Describes how the measuring device (heart rate frequency device) was chosen.

3. During the analyses of experimental data it became clear that the effects which were observed could not be summed together. ANOVA, Student's t and in general all the parametric statistical techniques require additive data. But data produced by retrocausal experiments is non-additive. This led to compare and test different statistical techniques.

5.1 Unpredictability of random sequences

In order to test anticipatory effects the fundamental condition is that the choice operated by the computer in phase 3 is unpredictable.

In a random sequence each term is totally independent from the previous and following terms, no rule links different parts of the sequence. This condition is known as unpredictability of random sequences and it is referred to as "lack of memory": the process of random selection does not recall any information about the values which were selected previously and cannot be used for the prediction of the values which will be selected in the future.

Random sequences imply the following qualities:

1. *Unpredictability.* The knowledge of any portion of the random sequence does not provide useful information in order to predict the outcome of any other element of the sequence. In other words, the knowledge of the first k values does not provide any element in order to predict the value k+1: this property is called unpredictability.
2. *Equiprobability.* A sequence is random if in each position each value has the same probability to be selected. In the case of a dice, each side has the same probability to be selected. Similarly, equal probability is expected when using a coin: during each tossing heads and tails have the same probability. Equiprobability implies independent sequences as it requires that the outcome of each selection is independent from any previous selection.
3. *Irregularity.* Unpredictability requires random sequences to be irregular and not repetitive.
4. *Absence of order.* In random sequences no type of structure or order can be detected.

The basic difference between *causal* and *random* can be traced back to the fact that *causal* events can be predicted, whereas *random* events cannot be predicted. As a consequence a random sequence can be defined as a sequence that no cognitive process will ever be able to predict.

5.2 Pseudorandom and random

Computer languages usually use the word random to identify the instruction which starts the algorithm for random selections of numbers.

In this work the Delphi-Pascal programming language was used. Delphi-Pascal has a predefined random sequence (2^{32} numbers) which can be assessed through a pointer which can be defined by the user or by the value of the built-in clock.

Delphi-Pascal uses the following instructions:

1. *Randomize* reads the value of the built-in clock and uses this value as the pointer to the predefined random sequence;
2. *Random* reads the value of the predefined sequence using the pointer selected by the randomize instruction.

The user can also define a personalized pointer. This option is generally used in software which encrypt information. Utilizing the same pointer the selection of random numbers from the predefined random sequence will always be the same.

It is important to understand why the random sequences produced by computers are named pseudorandom.

In order to obtain different random sequences the randomize procedure is used; this procedure reads the built-in clock of the computer in order to select an unpredictable pointer. The problem arises when the randomize procedures are recalled in a loop. As a consequence of the fact that each loop requires always the same processing time the new value selected from the built-in clock will be determined by the previous selection. In other words the selections, even if performed using a predefined random sequence, are all determined by the first value which was selected: the first value determines the second value, and so on, and the condition of independency between the selection of different terms is not met.

Usually the fact that the sequences generated by computers are pseudorandom is considered of secondary importance. However, in experiments which want to test anticipation, and which are based on the assumption of unpredictability, a pseudorandom sequence would inevitably be considered an artifact in the experimental design.

Luckily the solution to this problem is incredibly simple. The problem arises from the fact that the duration of the loops is always the same. In order to overcome this problem, obtaining in this way pure random selection, it is necessary to use loops which are based on unpredictable periods of time.

This condition can be easily met when an external, unpredictable factor, is inserted in the loop and modifies its execution time.

In the experiments conducted in this study, subject were asked to press a button corresponding to the color that he/she thinks the computer will select, the reaction time of the subject is always unpredictable. In this way, the unpredictable reaction time of the subject, makes the loop time become unpredictable, and the value selected from the built-in clock of the computer becomes independent from the other values previously selected.

In this way the independence among different selections is restored and the sequence becomes totally unpredictable: perfectly random.

For this reason, in all the experiments subjects were asked to guess; the real reason for this request was that of restoring the independence of the terms in the random sequence.

5.3 Choice of the heart rate frequency device

An assessment of the devices used to measure the parameters of the ANS system was carried out in late 2007. Most devices showed big problems in associating the measurements with the exact time, for the following reasons:

1. Many devices use a different clock from that used by the computer during the execution of the experiment.
2. The information saved on the file is not corrected according to the delay of the measurements.
3. Errors within instruments.

Producers and distributors of laboratory devices have been contacted, but all the products used built-in software which did not satisfy the synchronization requirements of the experiment. Furthermore the producers of these devices did not agree to provide the software keys which would allow the development of personalized software and the direct acquisition of heart rate data. The laboratory devices which have been assessed presented always these limits: proprietary software which did not allow to access directly the device. In order to try to overcome this limit a laboratory in North Italy provided some devices, and for each one the impossibility to establish a satisfactory synchronization between the device and the stimuli which were presented on the PC monitor was assessed.

In December 2007 the assessment was extended to devices used outside the experimental laboratories, in the field of sports training. Most devices showed the following limits:

1. Heart rate measurements are stored in a wrist watch, using in this way a different clock from the one used to conduct the experiment.
2. The information is stored without any compensation for the delay due to the measurement.
3. Some devices showed errors in the measurement.

After a long evaluation, the "home training" device produced by SUUNTO (www.suunto.com), was chosen. This system includes a thorax belt for measuring heart rate parameters, and a USB interface (PC-POD) which receives measurements by radio, using digital coded signals (which eliminate any possibility of interference) directly on the PC on which the experiment is carried out and using in this way the same clock of the experiment.

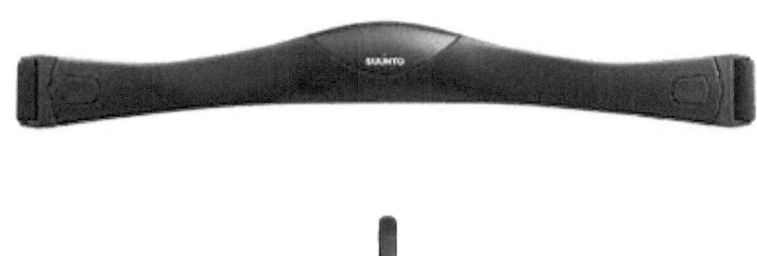

SUUNTO Heart rate monitor
consisting of a thorax belt and a USB radio receiver

The SUUNTO heart monitor device measured the heart frequency every second and saved this information in a file associated with the exact time (year, month, day, hour, minute and second). The measurement is relative to the average value during the second and is saved compensating the delay due to the time which is necessary to perform the measurement and to process the information. The heart rate data time, saved in the file, is therefore perfectly synchronized with the measurement performed.

The heart rate information is saved as an integer number, without any decimal values. The technical support unit of SUUNTO was contacted in Helsinki and gave full cooperation sending all the necessary documentation, software and .ddl libraries. They underlined that synchronization and precision of measurements are diverging parameters. A precise synchronization diminishes the precision of the measurement. A precision of heart rate units, synchronized at milliseconds can be considered an excellent measurement.

The SUUNTO "home training" device has been developed in order to monitor sports training activities and can be used in the most extreme conditions, for example underwater. It does not require the use of gel in order to conduct the signal and its use is extremely simple. Consequently it does not require the presence of an assistant in the same room in which the experiment is carried out. The only limit was observed in cold climates when the impossibility to measure the heart rate parameter was observed in some subjects. These subjects were excluded from the sample.

- Behavior of the SUUNTO heart rate device

Before starting the experiments the synchronization of the SUUNTO heart rate device with the clock of the PC was assessed. The heart rate information is shown in "real time" on the PC monitor and it is also saved in a file:

1. *In real time on the PC monitor.* In this modality it was observed that:
   A.   When the signal is deactivated (moving the device away from

the chest of the subject, point A) the measurement disappears after 5 seconds;

B. When the signal is reactivated (moving the device back on the chest of the subject, point B) the measurement reappears after 2 seconds.

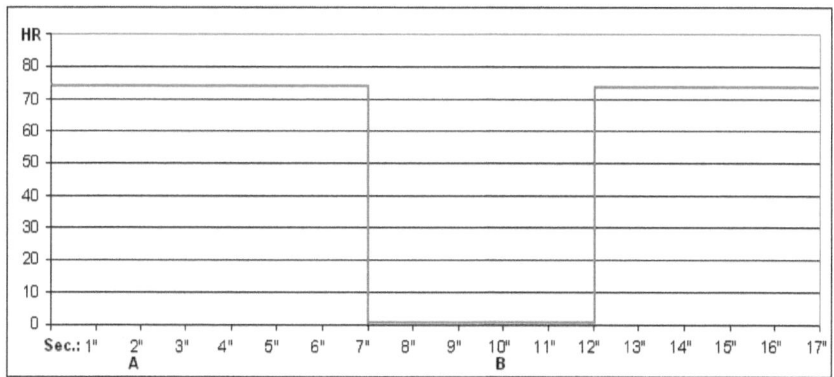

Behavior of SUUNTO heart rate measurements on the PC monitor

2. *Data saved in the file.* In this modality it was observed that:
    A. When the signal is deactivated (moving the device away from the chest of the subject, point A) the last measurement is kept for 3 seconds;
    B. When the signal is reactivated (moving the device back on the chest of the subject, point B) ***the measurement reappears immediately.***

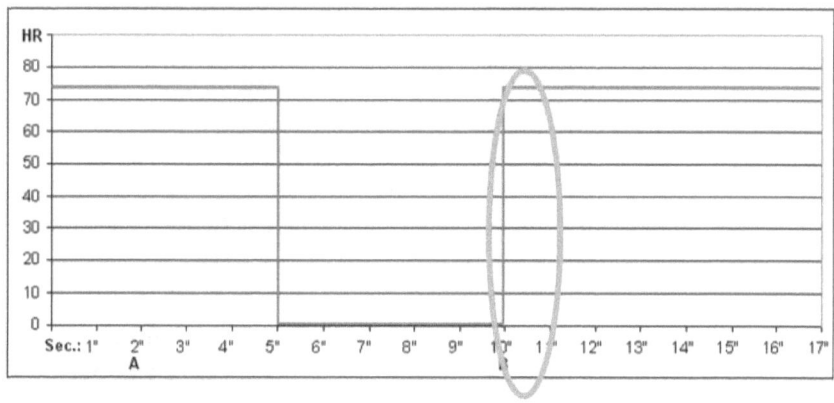

Behavior of SUUNTO heart rate measurements saved in the data file

This control shows that the delay in the measurements in "real time" on the PC monitor is approximately of 2 seconds, while in the data file the delay is compensated and the measurement is associated to the exact time (point B).

In the data file the measurement of the heart rate is associated with the time of the clock of the computer (year, month, day, hour, minute and second).

5.4 Stimuli

An experimental design divided in 3 phases was tested:

1. Stimuli are shown individually on the PC monitor and heart rate is measured.
2. Stimuli are shown together on the PC monitor and the subject is asked to guess which one will be selected by the computer.
3. The computer selects one of the 4 stimuli (target stimulus), using a random procedure, and shows it on the PC monitor full screen (feedback).

The first experiment was conducted using software developed in Visual Basic 2005. The following experiments used software developed in Delphi Pascal which allowed a better control of the computer hardware and a more precise synchronization of the presentation of the images.

The hypothesis of the experiment is that in the event of anticipatory effects heart rate measurements in phase 1 (the presentation phase) should be significantly different between target images (those which will be chosen by the computer in phase 3) and non-target images (those which will not be chosen by the computer).

The first experiments used stimuli made of black bars placed horizontally, vertically and diagonally on a white background. Data analysis did not show any significant difference between targets and non-targets.

The hypothesis was therefore analyzed in more depth and it was noticed that a key element of the "*syntropy retrocausal hypothesis*" is that anticipation is mediated by emotions and feelings and, therefore, in order to see differences between target and non-target stimuli, images should arise emotions.

Following this indication it was decided to use 4 elementary colors: blue, green, red and yellow. Using these colors, a strong difference in the heart frequencies between target and non-target stimuli was observed.

The difference was observed within the same colors, while considering all the colors together differences were not observed. It was therefore decided to conduct the experiments using these 4 elementary colors as stimuli.

Phases of an experimental trial are:

Phase 1 Presentation of stimuli and measurement of heart rate				Phase 2 Choice	Phase 3 Random selection
Blue	Green	Red	Yellow	Blue/Green/Red/Yellow	Red
					Target
4 seconds	*4 seconds*	*4 seconds*	*4 seconds*		*Feedback*

1. In phase 1 colors are presented on full screen for exactly 4 seconds and the heart rate is measured each second.
2. In phase 2 the experimental subject tries to guess the color which will be chosen by the computer.
3. In phase 3 the computer selects, using a random algorithm, one of the 4 colors (target) and shows it in full screen (feedback).

In the first experiment in phase 1, stimuli were presented for 4 seconds each. Heart rate was measured each second. In the second experiment, in phase 1, the duration of stimuli presentation was reduced to 2 seconds each.

This allowed to perform further controls on the behavior of the heart rate measurement device and the synchronization with the presentation of stimuli.

It is important to note that during the experiment two software are active:

1. The first software produced by SUUNTO for the processing of the heart rate information. This program was the Training Monitor 2.2.0 which associates each heart rate frequency to the date and second of the measurement. This data is stored in a file in a directory created by the SUUNTO software.

2. The second software was produced using Delphi Pascal for the presentation of stimuli and the conduction of the experiment. Stimuli were presented exactly at the turn of the second, with the precision of milliseconds, obtaining in this way a perfect synchronization between the data stored by the SUUNTO software and stimuli presented by the computer. The Delphi program saved data in a different directory from the one used by the SUUNTO program. Each event was associated with the exact moment of its happening (year, month, day, hour, minute, second and millisecond).

Only at the end of the experiment the two files were merged together using the time information.

5.5 Additive effects and statistical techniques

ANOVA is a collection of statistical models in which the observed variance is partitioned into components: *treatment variability* (between groups) and *error variability* (within groups).

The ratio of the treatment variability and the error variability produces a value, F, of which the statistical distribution is known and from which the statistical significance of the effect is obtained.

It is important to note some necessary conditions for the applicability of this statistical technique:

1. *Homoscedasticity*, according to which the variance of the groups which are selected should be the same. Greater variability of one group would result in false statistical significances.
2. *Additive effects*, according to which when effects are not additive the error variability tends to be greater and statistical significances are lost.

During the first experiment data analysis showed:

1. Strong statistically significant effects on all the colors, when the analysis was conducted within the same subject.
2. Effects disappeared or remained only on some colors when the analysis was carried out on the totality of the subjects.

Initially the idea was that the effect showed only on some colors because of specific characteristics of these colors; later it was understood that the effects vanished when the analysis was made globally as a consequence of the fact that the effect is non-additive.

Each subject presented a characteristic pattern in the reactions of the heart rate frequency.

For example, some subjects show an increase in the heart rate frequency when the target color is blue, and a reduction in the heart rate frequency when the target is green. Other subjects show a pattern which is exactly the opposite. Conducting the data analysis within each subject the retrocausal effect shows strong values of statistical significance. When, on the contrary, the analysis is carried out adding the effects observed among all the subjects, opposite effects subtract each other and a Type II error can be committed stating that no effect exists. Luckily, in the experiments the sample was always slightly unbalanced and the effect showed on some colors. Several controls were performed, modifying the sequence of presentation of colors and it was discovered that the effect appeared on all the colors.

In the last experiment the analysis was conducted using the Chi Square technique, and it was discovered that the effect could be observed always on all the colors. The absence of the effect, randomly on some colors, was the consequence of a statistical artefact due to the fact that ANOVA and generally all the parametric statistical techniques are not suited for dealing with non-additive effects.

When the effect cannot be added, because it is non-directional, the use of parametric statistical techniques leads to errors of type II, which consist in stating that an effect does not exist when it exists. These techniques are also particularly vulnerable to errors of type I which means stating that the effect exists when it does not exist. Errors of type I happen, for example, when an accidental value, out of scale, produces a statistical significance. On the contrary Chi Square operates on frequencies and each value has the same weight: out of scale values do not lead to false statistical significances.

The last experiment clearly shows that Chi Square and non-parametric techniques in general are more robust and allow to see more, reducing the risk of committing errors of first and second type.

Often in the field of psychology and neurosciences effects are non-directional and the use of ANOVA is not legitimate. It is therefore difficult to understand why in these fields ANOVA is nowadays, practically, the only technique used when operating statistical data analyses.

Raymond B. Cattel, well known in the field of statistics applied to psychology for its factor analysis techniques which are widely used, in the introduction of his book *"The Scientific use of Factor Analysis in Behavioral and Life Sciences"* (Cattell, 1976) noted that ANOVA was developed in order to answer the needs of American farmers and whereas the additive and homoscedasticity conditions can be met in the field of animal experimentation, rarely they can be satisfied when experiments are performed with humans.

In animal experimentation it is possible to use animals of the same weight and similar other characteristics. It is easy to have homogeneous groups and satisfy in this way the condition of homoscedasticity. Furthermore effects are generally directional.

On the contrary in the field of psychology it is difficult to have homogeneous samples and effects are often non-directional and therefore they do not satisfy the additive condition.

Historically ANOVA seems to have become popular because:

1. It was easy to calculate, even by hand. Before the 1980s computers were rarely available and ANOVA did not require the use of computers.
2. Experimental research in psychology is focused on animal experimentation. In this field it is possible to use ANOVA correctly because it is easier to have homogeneous samples and effects are usually directional.

This work suggests that the widespread use of t of Student and ANOVA has lead, in the field of experimental psychology, to unstable results characterized by low statistical significances.

6

PRE-STIMULI REACTIONS
OF HEART RATE MEASUREMENTS:
THE RETROCAUSAL EFFECT

In this chapter 3 experiments are described. Experimental conditions are gradually changed in order to understand better the characteristics of the effect.

The first experiment uses always, in phase 1, the same sequence of colors: blue, green, red and yellow. Subjects were given the task to try to guess the color that the computer would select, according to a random unpredictable procedure, in the last phase of the trial. If the retrocausal hypothesis is correct, differences in heart rate measurements in phase 1 should be observed between target stimuli (which will be later selected by the computer in phase 3) and non-target stimuli (those which will not be selected in phase 3). In the first experiment a sample of 24 subjects was used and results showed strong effects associated to the blue and green colors.

The second experiment was devised in order to answer the following questions:

1. The retrocausal effect is observed only on blue and green colors?
2. The retrocausal effect is observed only when using colors?
3. The retrocausal effect is observed only when the computer shows the feedback?

Results show that the effect is observed also on red and yellow colors according to their position in the sequence of colors used in phase 1; the effect is observed also when numbers are used instead of colors; the effect disappears when the computer does not show the feedback; the effect seems to be stronger when the stimulus is closer to the feedback, at the end of the presentation phase.

In this second experiment the control on the feedback was performed removing the feedback every 5 trials. This regularity could constitute an artifact. A third experiment was performed in which the feedback was removed randomly. Results show that when the feedback is shown strong differences are observed among target and non-target colors in phase 1, while when the target is not shown these differences disappear. This control removes the possibility that the difference among target and non-target colors could depend on causes which precede the choice operated by the computer (phase 3).

6.1 Experiment number 1

In the first experiments, stimuli were presented in phase 1 for 4 seconds each. Heart rate was measured each second.

Phase 1 Presentation of colors and measurement of heart rate				Phase 2 Choice	Phase 3 Random selection
Blue	Green	Red	Yellow	Blue/Green/Red/Yellow	Red
					Target
4 seconds	4 seconds	4 seconds	4 seconds		Feedback

Phases of an experimental trial

Each trial of the experiment was divided in 3 phases.

1. *Presentation phase*: 4 colors were presented one after the other on the screen of the computer: blue, green, red and yellow, for exactly 4 seconds each. The subject was asked to look at the colors, and the heart frequency was measured at fixed intervals of 1 second. For each color 4 measurements of the heart frequency were saved: one each second. The presentation of the color was perfectly synchronized with the heart rate measurement. When necessary the synchronization was re-established showing a white image before the presentation of the color. The SUUNTO heart frequency device did not require any type of supervision. Subjects were alone while conducting the experiment.

2. *Choice phase*: at the end of the presentation of the 4 colors, an image with 4 color bars was shown (blue, green, red and yellow) in order to allow the subject to choose (using the mouse) the color which he thinks the computer will select. In other words, the subject was asked to guess the color which the computer will select.
3. *Random selection of the target and feedback*: as soon as the subject chose a color the computer selected the target color, using a random process, and showed the selected color full-screen on the computer (feedback).

The experiment consisted of 20 trials and requires approximately 7 minutes. Each subject was asked to repeat the experiment 3 times.

6.1.2 Hypothesis

Target is the color selected and shown by the computer after the subject performs the guess.

The hypothesis is that in presence of a retrocausal effect differences should be observed between heart rates measured in phase 1 during the presentation of target colors and non-target colors.

6.1.3 Sample

The experiment was conducted on a sample of 24 subjects, with ages ranging from 15 to 75 years. A total of 14 females and 10 males was present in this sample.

Each subject performed the experiment 3 times, for a total time of slightly more than 20 minutes.

Heart rate frequency was measured 960 times for each subject, producing a sample of heart rate frequencies which allowed to calculate statistical significances also within each subject.

6.1.4 Results

Taking into account all the heart rate frequencies no significant difference was observed between target and non-target images; the target images obtained an average value of the heart rate frequency of 80.94 and the non-target images of 80.97. But, when the analysis was conducted within each color, strong differences of the heart rate were observed between targets and non-targets for the blue color (target 81.99 and non-target 79.84) and the green color (target 79.60 and non-target 81.45). These differences correspond to a t of Student value of 10.74 for the blue color, and 8.81 for the green color.

A t Student value of 3.291 is statistically significant with $p<0.001$, meaning that there is less than 1 probability out of 1,000 to be wrong when stating that the difference is not a product of chance. A t of Student of 8.81 (obtained comparing the target and non-target images of the green color) tells that the probability of being wrong is practically equal to zero; it is therefore possible to state, with almost absolute certainty, that there is a difference between target and non-target images, which is not a consequence of chance.

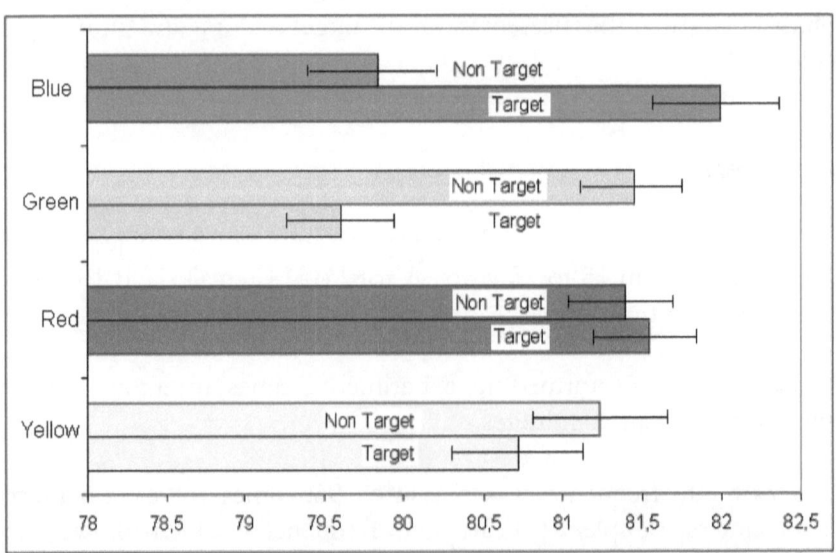

Mean heart rate frequency divided by color and target

A second analysis was performed using the Chi Square test. Statistical significance was calculated comparing the number of measurements which were over or under the baseline of the color. Also in this case a strong statistical significance was observed with Chi Square values over 30; $p < 0.001$ statistical significance is reached with Chi Square values of 10.8.

6.1.5 Discussion

Even though a strong anticipated heart rate difference was observed, no ability of the subjects to guess the target was noticed. As a whole, 26.8% of the total guesses were correct, one out of 4, which is what we would expect by chance. In other words the rational conscious side seems unable to access the anticipatory information which is observed with the heart frequency measurements.

It is also important to underline that strong individual differences were observed. While most subjects showed a tendency towards higher heart rate frequencies when blue was target and lower heart rate frequencies when green was target, two subjects showed strong results in the opposite direction.

Using parametric statistical techniques, such as t of Student and ANOVA, in which values are added, opposite significant effects are subtracted resulting in a null effect, leading to a Type II error: which means stating that the effect does not exist when it exists.

For example, in the colors red and yellow statistically significant effects were observed within the subjects, but these effects were diverging and in the general analysis they canceled each other, leading to state that no effect exists on the yellow and on the red colors.

6.1.6 Control of artifacts

Artifacts are systematic errors which lead to observe effects which do not exist. Sometimes artifacts are used intentionally by the experimenter in order to reach the desired results; other times they consist in simple errors which produce accidental effects.

For example:

1. Errors linked to the experimental design are often caused by intervening variables which have not been controlled. For instance, if in the experimental group the treatment is a substance, a drug in the form of a pill, while the control group does not receive any substance (no placebo pill), at the end of the experiment it will be impossible to say if the observed effect was caused by the substance in the pill or by the placebo effect of the pill.
2. Errors can be caused by non-homogeneous groups. Experiments are usually based on the comparison of groups, for example those who have received a drug and those who have received a placebo. The attribution to groups is randomized in order to distribute equally all the characteristics of the population in the groups. However, in order to obtain homogeneous groups, randomization requires samples with a high number of subjects. Experiments are often conducted on small size samples, and characteristics such as instruction, income, health, are not equally distributed among groups. In a group a higher proportion of highly educated subjects could cause differences among groups. These differences can be erroneously attributed to the "experimental treatment" when, instead, they are a consequence of differences of sample variables.
3. Errors linked with the measuring device happen when measurements are performed in systematically different ways among groups. When this happens differences observed can be the consequence of the different way measurements were performed. In this case a systematic error of measuring is the cause of the effect.
4. Errors linked to statistical data analyses. Statistical techniques can be affected by extreme values and the differences observed can

be the consequence of these extreme values and not of the effect; furthermore, data might not comply with the requirements of the technique: this happens frequently when using parametric techniques which require the Gaussian distribution of data and additive effects.

5. Errors can be linked to intentional manipulation of data by the experimenter in order to obtain the desired results.

In this work the control of these possible artifacts has been operated in the following ways:

1. *Experimental design.* The experiment is designed in such a way that the only element which differs is the quality of the stimuli presented in phase 3: target or non-target (selected or non-selected by the computer). All the other conditions remain the same. It is therefore possible to state that the effect which is observed cannot be caused by any other variable, as no other variables exist which might be associated to the target or non-target condition of the stimulus during presentation.

2. *Sampling.* Differently from other experiments in which the sample is divided in the experimental group and the control group, in this experiment the distinction between target and non-target stimuli is made within the same sample of subjects. This experimental design does not require, therefore, the randomization of the sample. Measurements cannot be affected by sample differences as the sample used is always the same.

3. *Systematic measurement errors.* The measurement of heart rate frequencies is performed in the same identical way when target or non-target images are shown. No other variable associated with the measurement of heart rates frequencies during target and non-target images exists. Consequently no systematic error of measurement can be associated to target and non-target stimuli.

4. *Statistical analysis of data.* Statistical analysis is always a very tricky field which hides problems of which the researcher is often not aware. In the last experiment statistical data analyses are performed using non-parametric techniques, because the requirements for the use of parametric techniques cannot be met. Statistical artifacts are quite frequent when using parametric techniques. These techniques can lead to Type I and II errors

because of extreme values or non-directional effects. These errors are impossible when using non-parametric statistical techniques, based on the comparison of frequencies. Furthermore, non-correlated targets (generated by the computer, but not shown to the subjects) were used in order to assess the validity of the statistical analysis. This control eliminated the doubt that statistical significances, which were observed, could be a product of chance.

5. *Intentional manipulation of data and results by the experimenter.* Often, in order to participate to a congress, experimenters manipulate data sets in such a way that statistical significant results are obtained. The doubt of data manipulation remains as long as the same results are not replicated by other researchers.

About the heart rate device, the SUUNTO device used in these experiments has a range which goes from 30 heart rate beats per minute to 230 heart rate beats per minute, with a measuring error of ±0.5. One of the fundamental laws is that measuring errors distribute themselves randomly, according to a Gaussian curve, around the mean values. This law is known as the law of the sampling distribution of means states that:

"the mean of the means of samples, coincides with the mean of the population from which the samples were selected."

While a single measurement has an error of ±0.5 beats per minute, repeated measurements result in a reduced error. In the experiments conducted in this study, the number of measurements performed allows to consider significant digit of mean values up to the fourth decimal. Anyhow, the last experiment data analysis has been performed using non parametric techniques (Chi Square and Fisher's exact test) which do not require the comparison of mean values.

As it will be seen these techniques lead to extremely significant results, and do not require the precision of measurements which parametric techniques require.

Furthermore, data analyses performed on single subjects show that variations in heart rate measurements between target and non-target stimuli can be very strong (up to 10 beats per minute), and this fact eliminates any requirement for a measurement device which can be precise up to the hundredth of a heartbeat.

Generally speaking, the problem of the measuring device is assessed when no significant results are observed and it is therefore suggested that the problem can be caused by the measurement device.

In this study strong and statistically significant effects are observed and these effects replicate each time.

6.2 Experiment number 2

The second experiment was performed in order to answer the following questions:

1. Is the retrocausal effect observed only on blue and green colors?
2. Is the retrocausal effect observed only using colors?
3. Is the retrocausal effect observed only when the computer shows the feedback in phase 3?

The experiment was organized in 5 different types of trials:

1. In 3 trials the sequence of the colors was varied, in order to answer question n. 1.
2. In one trial instead of colors numbers were used, in order to answer question n. 2.
3. In one trial the feedback was not shown, in order to answer question n. 3.

The effect is assessed again in the form of differences between heart rates measured in phase 1 during the presentation of target colors and non-target colors.

6.2.1 Hypothesis

The following hypothesis were formulated.

1. The retrocausal effect is expected in all the trials in which the target is shown. Showing the target is considered to be the cause of the heart rate effect.
2. The retrocausal effect is expected on all the colors. The hypothesis is that the retrocausal effect is transported by emotions and it is believed that all colors, and also stimuli different from colors, can have an emotional content.
3. The retrocausal effect is based on the hypothesis of anticipated waves which move backward in time. It is therefore expected a stronger effect closer to the feedback, during the presentation of stimuli at the end of phase 1, closer to phase 3.

6.2.2 Procedure

The experiment was based on 5 different trials, each one with a different sequence of colors and stimuli:

1. in phase 1 of the first trial the sequence is blue, green, red and yellow and each color is presented for 4 seconds; in phase 2 the computer shows all the colors together and waits for the choice operated by the subject; in phase 3 the computer randomly selects the target color and shows it full screen. A button is shown with the percentage of times the subject has guessed correctly; the subject has to press the button in order to start a new trial.
2. in phase 1 of the second trial the sequence is yellow, red, green and blue and each color is presented for 4 seconds; in phase 2 the computer shows all the colors together and waits for the choice operated by the subject; in phase 3 the computer randomly selects the target color and shows it full screen. A button is shown with the percentage of times the subject has guessed correctly; the subject has to press the button in order to start a new trial.
3. in phase 1 of the third trial the sequence is green, blue, yellow and

red and each color is presented for 4 seconds; in phase 2 the computer shows all the colors together and waits for the choice operated by the subject; in phase 3 the computer randomly selects the target color and shows it full screen. A button is shown with the percentage of times the subject has guessed correctly; the subject has to press the button in order to start a new trial.

4. in phase 1 of the fourth trial the sequence is blue, green, red and yellow and each color is presented for 4 seconds; in phase 2 the computer shows all the colors together and waits for the choice operated by the subject; in phase 3 the computer randomly selects the target color but does not show the selected color (*no feedback*). A button is shown with the percentage of times the subject has guessed correctly; the subject has to press the button in order to start a new trial.

5. in phase 1 of the fifth trial the sequence is no. 1, no. 2, no. 3 and no. 4 and each number is presented for 4 seconds; in phase 2 the computer shows all the numbers together and waits for the choice operated by the subject; in phase 3 the computer randomly selects the target number and shows it full screen. A button is shown with the percentage of times the subject has guessed correctly; the subject has to press the button in order to start a new trial.

This sequence of 5 trials was repeated for 20 times, reaching a total of 100 trials for each subject, for a total length of the experiment of slightly more than 45 minutes.

Heart rate was measured throughout all the experiments every second.

6.2.3 Sample

The sample was of 23 subjects, 14 females and 8 males, ranging from 16 to 61 years of age. The experiment consisted of 100 trials, 20 for each type, and required slightly more than 40 minutes.

For each color in phase 1 only one measurement of the heart rate was used in the statistical data analysis. The number of heart rate measurements is therefore 400 (for each subject) x 23 (subjects) = 9,200 (Total).

6.2.4 Results

The effect was studied using the t of Student test and was assessed as differences between heart rate measurements (taken in phase 1) in association with target and non-target stimuli (determined in phase 3).

In this experiment strong differences were observed, with t Student values greater than 6.

Briefly, results show that:

1. Colors behave in different ways according to their position and the effect is not always on the blue and green colors.
2. The effect is stronger at the end of phase 1.
3. The effect appears also when numbers, instead of colors are used (in this experiments numbers from 1 to 4 were used).
4. When the feedback is not shown the effect disappears.

The data analysis was carried out twice, once considering the second heart rate measured during the stimulus presentation, and the second time considering the third heart rate (4 heart rates were measured for each stimulus). In both data analyses 400 heart rate measurements were taken into account for each subject. As a whole the total number of cases (n) was 400 x 23 = 9,200. The difference among the heart rates was studied using the t of Student test. This test reaches statistical significance of:

1. 5% - with values equal or exceeding 1.96;
2. 1% - with values equal or exceeding 2.576;
3. 1/1000 – with values equal or exceeding 3.291.

The following table shows a strong statistical significance for targets placed in the last position, just before the feedback. Heart rate measurements go from an average of 78.78, observed for non-targets, to 80.37, observed for targets.

Statistical significant differences between targets and non-targets using the t of Student (first 3 trials)	
1° position	-
2° position	-
3° position	-
4° position	6.445

In the last position a statistically significant difference
of p<0.001 (t of student 6.445) was observed

As noticed in the previous two experiments the effect tends to counterbalance on different colors; in some colors and positions an increases in the measurement of the heart rate is observed, in other colors and positions a decrease is observed. The effect is also observed in the 5th trial, in which numbers were presented instead of colors.

Next table shows that the effect on colors changes according to their position in the sequence. It is important to remember that while in the first 3 trials the computer shows the feedback, in the fourth trial the feedback is not shown. In this last trial no statistically significant differences were observed between target and non-target colors. This result confirms the fact that when the feedback is not shown (in phase 3) the effect (in phase 1) disappears.

	Trial with colors			
	1	2	3	4
Blue	-	4.746	-3.455	-
Green	-	-	2.839	-
Red	-6.649	-	-	-
Yellow	5.623	-3.894	-	-

Differences between targets and non-targets
measured with t of Student

The absence of the effect in the fourth trial leads to the exclusion of causes which could be previous to the effect. The hypothesis of an anticipatory effect seems to be the only possible conclusion.

The fifth trial shows a strong effect (t of Student -5.7) only on targets associated to the last position (number 4). This result supports the hypothesis that the effect is stronger when the stimulus is closer to the feedback.

6.2.5 Discussion

It is important to note that in the first trial of this experiment, which is identical to the trial used in the first experiment, statistically significant results are associated to the red and yellow colors and not to blue and green, as it was the case in the first experiment. In the first experiment it was noted that the effects observed within the subjects, and which are strongly significant from a statistical point of view, often have opposite directions among subjects. Therefore, when they are added together they tend to cancel and disappear and only the configuration which accidentally happens to be more represented remains statistically significant. This consideration shows how dangerous the use of techniques like mean values, t of Student and ANOVA can be.

In this experiment two controls have been added:

1. Non correlated trials were added to the data analysis in order to assess if statistical significances could happen by chance. Data analyses showed that these uncorrelated targets were not associated with significant differences in the heart rate frequencies measured in phase 1.
2. The probability of choosing a target is always the same, and each stimulus should at the end show a frequency distribution similar to the others. In this experiment, as was also done in the other experiments, it was checked if the distribution of the targets is flat. Distribution data show that the blue was chosen as a target 547 times, green 591, red 563 and yellow 599. This distribution meets the expectations of a random sequence.

Differences emerged between the data which was collected in the experiments conducted in the laboratory of the Department of Psychology in Rome and experiments conducted at home. Statistical significance is stronger in the data collected at home, and subjects in the experiments conducted in the laboratory of the Department of Psychology showed a tendency to guess less correctly.

While at home subjects guessed on an average correctly more than 26%, in the laboratory of Psychology the percentage dropped to 23%.

These results seems to support the hypothesis that emotionally resonant environments can favor the propagation of signals based on emotions and therefore reinforce the retrocausal effect.

6.3 Experiment number 3

In the second experiment the control on the feedback was performed removing the feedback every 5 trials. This regularity could constitute an artifact. A third experiment was performed in which the feedback was removed randomly. Results show that when the feedback is shown strong differences are observed among target and non-target colors in phase 1, whereas when the target is not shown these differences disappear. This control rules out the possibility that the difference between target and non-target colors can depend on causes which precede the choice operated by the computer.

6.3.1 Procedure

This experiment differs from the first one for two elements:

1. the computer chooses in a totally random way if the feedback will be shown or not.
2. The presentation of stimuli in phase 1 was reduced from 4 seconds to 2 seconds. This condition allowed to increase the

number of heart rate measurements which could be used in the statistical data analyses and reduce the length of the experiment.

6.3.2 Hypothesis

The experiment was intended to:

1. Verify again the retrocausal effect in phase 1.
2. Verify if the effect in phase 1 persists when the feedback is not shown. More precisely when the computer selects the color (phase 3), but instead of showing the selected color a grey full screen is shown.

According to the Fantappiè and King's model the hypothesis is that when the feedback is not shown the retrocausal effect should not show either.

6.3.3 Sample

The experiment consisted of 100 trials per subject, of which slightly less than 1 out of 5 were without feedback. The sample consisted of 8 subjects. Trials without feedback were chosen randomly by the computer. On a total of 800 trials 151 were without feedback, of 3,200 heart rate measurements (8 subjects x 100 trials x 4 stimuli) 604 were without feedback and 2,596 with feedback.

6.3.4 Results

Even though the presentation time was reduced from 4 to 2 seconds the effect emerged with strong statistical differences within the blue and the yellow colors when the feedback was shown (trials with feedback).

On the other hand, the effect was totally absent when the computer, after performing the choice of the target color, did not show it on the monitor (trials without feedback).

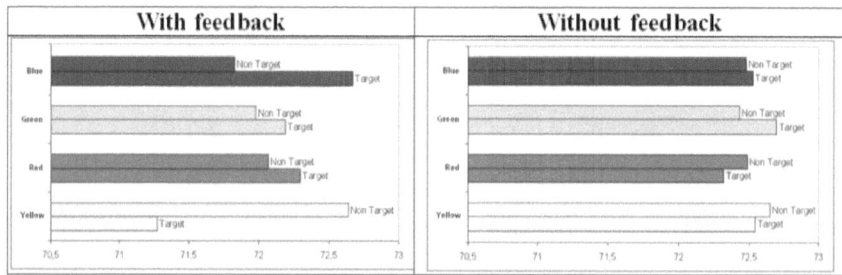

Average heart rate values

6.3.4 Discussion

It is interesting to note that in the first experiment the effect was strong with the blue and green colors, while in this second experiment the effect on the green color was absent but was present on the yellow color. As it will be shown in the last experiment, this modulation is a consequence of the fact that effects are not additive and when using mean values, t of Student or ANOVA subjects which show the effect, but in different directions, cancel each other.

In this experiment, as in the previous one, a slight tendency towards guessing correctly the outcome was noticed (26% compared to 25% which was expected). This difference is not statistically significant, but it is interesting to note that while in the first 50 trials 25.08% of the guesses were correct, in the last 50 trials this percentage increases to 26.95%. This increase suggests the existence of a learning process.

	First 50 trials	Last 50 trials	Total
Guessed	25.08%	26.95%	26.04%
Not guessed	74.92%	73.05%	73.96%
Total	100.00%	100.00%	100.00%
	(315)	(334)	(649)

Outcome of the guessing task in trials with feedback

If this learning effect is confirmed, it would support the hypothesis that subjects can learn to listen to their emotional signals and use them in order to favor positive outcomes.

127

From a cognitive point of view learning to guess correctly should be simply impossible in an experiment, like this one, in which the selection performed by the computer is totally unpredictable.

7

ROLE OF EMOTIONS IN DECISION MAKING

Damasio and Bechara (Damasio, 1994) formulated a dual system of processing of information, on which decision making would be based:

1. *Conscious system*, or declaratory, which uses verbal processes of reasoning in order to formulate decisions;
2. *Emotional system*, unconscious, non-declaratory, which uses a different neurophysiological network in which Somatic Markers, which can be measured through skin conductance and heart rate frequencies, seem to play a key role.

Damasio did not consider the possibility that anticipatory reactions observed in gambling, using skin conductance, could be the result of real *anticipation* and not only of learning.

The design of his experiments is based on implicit rules which do not allow to distinguish the retrocausal and learning component of the anticipatory reactions.

The syntropic model of consciousness suggests that decision making uses:

1. *Cognitive information*, implicit and explicit, which follow the classical flow of information, from the past to the future, and are based on the use of memory, learning and experience.
2. *Retrocausal information*, based on the perception of emotional signals, which follow the backwards flow of information, from the future to the past, and take the form of signals associated to the autonomic nervous system (ANS).

7.1 Role of emotions in decision making

Studying neurological patients affected by decision making deficits, Damasio suggested the hypothesis, known as the hypothesis of the somatic markers (SM), that emotions are part of the network of reasoning and constitute a part of the decision making process, instead of opposing it.

According to Damasio, emotions allow to operate advantageous choices, without having to produce advantageous assessments.

Damasio suggests that during evolution, cognitive processes were added to emotional processes, maintaining the centrality of emotions in decision making. This hypothesis would be supported by the fact that when in danger, when choices need to be done quickly, reasoning is bypassed. Damasio uses the example of fear, an emotion which allows people to make instantaneous decisions in order to avoid risks, in which the role of reasoning is limited.

The study of neurological patients affected by decision making deficits shows that the processes which usually are judged necessary and sufficient for rational processes are intact. Tests show that the following functions are totally functioning: short and long term memory, operational memory, attention, perception, language, abstract logic, arithmetical abilities, intelligence, learning, the knowledge of elements which constitute the problem on which it is necessary to operate a decision and the system of values.

These subjects respond in a normal way to the majority of tests and their cognitive functions are undamaged: intelligence, perception, memory, learning, language, arithmetic, attention and mental plasticity. They show normal intellect, but are unable to decide in an appropriate way for their future.

A dissociation between the ability to decide advantageously and the ability to decide for objects, numbers and space is observed.

In neuropsychology this deficit is described as dissociation between cognitive abilities and their use. On one side the cognitive abilities are undamaged, on the other side the patient is not able to use them advantageously for the future.

This dissociation also takes the form of reduced links between the abstract system of values and the real life.

Studying neurological patients Damasio discovered that deficits in decision making were always accompanied by alterations in emotions and in the ability to feel emotional states.

According to Damasio, the use of reasoning strategies depends, to a large extent, on the ability to feel emotions.

Damasio suggests that during evolution the strategies of reasoning developed guided by biological mechanisms of regulation, of which emotions and feelings are important aspects. This hypothesis does not contradict the fact that emotions and feelings can sometime cause disorders in the reasoning processes, but underlines the extraordinary fact that the absence of emotions and feelings can be even more damaging.

While all the cognitive functions of patients with decision making deficits are intact, the ability to feel emotions is visibly altered: antisocial behavior can be observed, behaviors against ethics and cold reasoning are common.

These patients are always neutral in respect to emotions: with never a shade of sadness, no impatience or frustration. The absence of emotional reactions, positive or negative, is observed.

Furthermore, subjects affected by decision making deficits show a behavior which can be described as *"short sighted toward the future"*.

Damasio underlines that this same deficit affects those who are under the effect of alcohol or drugs.

In other words, the absence of emotions leads to the inability to perform advantageous decisions.

Damasio observed: no worry about the future, the inability to plan the future, the inability to produce efficient plans for the coming hours, confusion about priorities, the absence of intuitions and the absence of any trace of precognition.

These patients also show maniacality in the execution of tasks, not correlated with their future, inability to learn from their errors, compromised free will and compromised independence.

On the contrary subjects who put forward advantageous strategies for their future show emotions which help to decide in accordance with a feeling for their future, which help to orient rationality in the correct direction, leading to the appropriate decisions in which it is possible to use correctly the instruments of logic. This helps to forecast an uncertain future and organize actions. It activates experiences of precognitions, which favor ethical judgments and the harmonization of individual behavior with social conventions.

Damasio considers advantageous any decision which favors survival of the individual, of the family, and which favors the satisfaction of primary needs such as shelter, health, work, financial situation, and a good collocation in the social group.

7.2 Decision making deficit and the prefrontal cortex

In these subjects decisional deficit cannot be attributed to damages to any cognitive process; instead it seems located in the most advanced stages of reasoning, in proximity with the point where decisions are taken and where answers emerge.

Damasio noted that specific lesions of the prefrontal cortex (PFC), especially in those sectors which integrate signals arriving from the body and which generate maps, lead to the absence or the imperfect perception of somatic feelings linked to emotions. Damasio says that these subjects are characterized *by knowing but not by feeling.*

After prefrontal cortex impairments, emotions and feelings are compromised and patients lose the ability to choose the most advantageous direction, even if mental abilities are intact.

Feelings involved in decision making processes are:

1. heart feelings, in the form of accelerated heart beat;
2. lungs, in the form of contraction of breath;
3. intestines;
4. muscles.

Emotions, feelings, biological regulation all have a place in human reasoning. The most modest levels of our organism take part in the higher processes of reasoning. In the neural construction of reasoning, the lower levels are the same as those which regulate the processing of emotions and feelings, together with the somatic information which is necessary for the survival of the organism.

Decision making deficits are also observed:

1. in those patients in which prefrontal leucotomy was performed. Extreme anxiety vanishes, but also their emotions and brain activities which caused compulsions and delirium vanish. These patients become calm, they don't suffer any longer, but their ability to decide and to act is compromised.
2. Patients who are not able to recognize objects, who are not able to make plans for their future or to make decisions for their personal life, show difficulties in the perception of their emotional state.

Neurological damages associated to decision making deficits suggest that coherent systems dedicated to reasoning toward the future exist in the brain. These systems would be goal oriented, moved by finalities, and would be at the basis of reasoning processes and the production of answers and decision making. These systems seem to be involved also in emotions and in the processing of feelings and body signals.

Damasio suggests that the areas in the right region of the brain produce, thanks to their interactions, integrated maps of the state and feelings of the body, and this makes them indispensable for the perception of emotional feelings which come from the heart, lungs, intestine and muscles.

After observing patents with front lesions of the brain Damasio suggested that in this area emotions, feelings, attention and memory interact, becoming the main source of outer movement and inner movement (reasoning). Patients with lesions in this area show a suspended movement. A damage in this area not only limits movements, attention and emotions, but also suspends the processes of reasoning, and reasoning is no more used.

Between the "low" old brain structure and the "high" new structures there is such a great difference that generally it is believed that they have different roles: the old structures would be involved in biological regulations, while the new structures would be involved in rational processes and thinking. At the higher levels will and reasoning occur, while at the low levels emotions take place.

On the contrary, the study of patients with decision making deficits, shows that rationality and will, generally considered to be placed in the high cortical levels, do not take place without emotions, generally considered subcortical; it seems that nature has built the cortical structures not just over the subcortical one, but starting from this and interacting with it.

7.3 Decision making as a process oriented to the future

Deciding well also means deciding quickly, especially when the time factor is essential, or at least deciding within a time frame which is adequate to the problem to be faced.

Rational decision making are too long, much longer than that which is acceptable if in the same day it is necessary to operate many decisions.

Calculating costs and benefits is slow and often inconclusive. Why? Because it is not simple to keep track of all the possible levels of gains and losses which need to be compared.

Damasio states that rationality cannot function as a decision making process, it requires too much time and it is not oriented towards the future. Therefore when only rational processes are available the person does not arrive at the formulation of any decision.

The experience with neurological patients with decision making impairment suggests that the cold strategy of rationality describes the way in which patients affected by prefrontal damages behave in order to decide, and not the way in which normal subjects behave when they have to take a decision.

Damasio arrives at the conclusion that having a mind means having representations and images which can be manipulated in a reasoning process in order to influence our decision to forecast the future and plan the best actions and choices. Damasio recalls the words of Blaise Pascal:

"We think very little of time present; we anticipate the future" and *"the heart has its reasons which reason knows nothing of."*

Pascal's words show the virtual inexistence of the present.

The decision making process is always oriented to the future.

Reasoning and decision making are relative to this continuous and all-inclusive process of anticipation and creation of the future.

In order to decide we need to have some kind of strategy which produces reliable inferences about the future, on which to base an adequate response, and that processes which support reasoning are functioning.

This strategy seems to be based on emotions and feelings.

7.4 The hypothesis of the somatic marker

When talking about decision making usually the reference is to attention and memory and rarely to emotions and feelings.

Damasio's hypothesis, known as the hypothesis of the somatic marker, is that when the negative outcome of a decision comes to our mind a negative feeling is felt in the stomach. Because this feeling is relative to the body, Damasio named it with the technical name "somatic state"; and because it marks an image, he used the word marker.

What is the role of somatic markers? According to Damasio they force attention towards the negative outcome of a specific choice, and act as an alarm signal which says: "*warning your choice is dangerous.*" This signal can help to abandon immediately the negative path which has been chosen and choose more appropriately. This does not exclude the cost/benefits analysis, but only after the reduction of possible alternatives operated by somatic markers. Somatic markers transform decision making into a much faster, efficient and precise process, while their absence reduces the efficiency and precision of decision making.

Damasio suggests that somatic markers are linked through experience and learning to the ability of predicting future outcomes. When a negative somatic marker is associated to a future outcome it works as an alarm bell; when a positive somatic marker is associated to a future outcome it enlightens the options.

According to Damasio somatic markers are acquired with experience, under the influence of the outside world and the inner world.

In the first phases of development, parents and the outer world interact with the baby through punishments and rewards according to which ethics, culture and social rules are acquired.

When the outcome of a choice is punishment, and pain, the system of the somatic markers acquires this information.

During development the great majority of decision making processes is formed through somatic states which are correlated to rewards and punishments.

According to Damasio, will is moved by an immediate state of suffering and the prospect of a better future state; it would therefore be based on present suffering in view of an improved state of being.

The "force of will" would therefore be a different name used to describe a decision making process characterized by long-term choices. In other words decision making is made comparing the present state of suffering with the future rewards and also with possible greater suffering.

7.5 Intuition

Damasio describes intuition as that mysterious process through which we arrive at the solution of a problem without thinking about it. Damasio recalls the words of the mathematician Poincaré which he considers coherent with the model of the somatic markers:

"The genesis of mathematical creation is a problem which should intensely interest the psychologist. To invent is to choose; but the word is perhaps not wholly exact. It makes one think of a purchaser before whom are displayed a large number of samples, and who examines them, one after the other, to make a choice. In mathematics the samples would be so numerous that a whole lifetime would not suffice to examine them. This is not the actual state of things. The sterile combinations do not even present themselves to the mind of the inventor. Never in the field of his consciousness do combinations appear that are not really useful, except some that he rejects but which have to some extent the characteristics of useful combinations. All goes on as if the inventor were an examiner for the second [academic] degree who would only have to question the candidates who had passed a previous examination. (...) For fifteen days I strove to prove that there could not be any functions like those I have since called Fuchsian functions. I was then very ignorant; every day I seated myself at my work table, stayed an hour or two, tried a great number of combinations and reached no results. One evening, contrary to my custom, I drank black coffee and could not sleep. Ideas rose in

crowds; I felt them collide until pairs interlocked, so to speak, making a stable combination. By the next morning I had established the existence of a class of Fuchsian functions, those which came from the hypergeometric series; I had only to write out the results, which took but a few hours. Just at this time I left Caen, where I was then living, to go on a geologic excursion under the auspices of the school of mines. The changes of travel made me forget my mathematical work. We entered an omnibus to go someplace or other. At the moment when I put my foot on the step the idea came to me, without anything in my former thoughts seeming to have paved the way for it, that the transformations I had used to define the Fuchsian functions were identical with those of non-Euclidean geometry. I did not verify the idea; I should not have had time, as upon taking my seat in the omnibus, I went on with a conversation already commenced, but I felt a perfect certainty. On my return to Caen, for conscience's sake, I verified the result at my leisure. (...) One morning, walking on the bluff, the idea came to me, with just the same characteristics of brevity, suddenness and immediate certainty, that the arithmetic transformations of indeterminate ternary quadratic forms were identical with those of non-Euclidean geometry. (...) Thereupon I left for Mont-Valerian, where I was to go through my military service; so I was very differently occupied. One day, going along the street, the solution of the difficulty which had stopped me suddenly appeared to me. I did not try to go deep into it immediately, and only after my service did I again take up the question. I had all the elements and had only to arrange them and put them together. So I wrote out my final memoir at a single stroke and without difficulty."

The conclusions to which Poincaré arrived are similar to those suggested by Damasio, in the way that it is not necessary to apply reasoning to all possible options, because some kind of pre-selection takes place. Some type of mechanism operates this selection, and allows only a limited number of possibilities to reach the final examination.

According to Leo Szilard:

"Scientists have a lot in common with artists and poets. Logic and analytical thinking are necessary attributes of the scientist, but are not sufficient for a creative work. In science intuitions which have led to progress are not logically derived from pre-existing knowledge: creative processes on which the progress of science is based operate at an unconscious level."

7.6 Somatic markers and autonomic nervous system (ANS)

In the perspective of evolution it seems that the autonomic nervous system is the means by which the brain of simple organisms regulates the internal functions of the body.

When life functions were limited to supporting few organs, and when the type and number of interactions with the environment was limited, ANS governed the majority of the functions. What the brain required was some type of signal about the state of the different organs and a way in order to modify their state according to specific circumstances.

ANS was providing exactly this: an input and output network.

The autonomic nervous system, also known as visceral nervous system, is the part of the peripheral nervous system that acts as a control system functioning largely below the level of consciousness, and controls visceral functions. ANS affects heart rate, digestion, respiration rate, salivation, perspiration, diameter of the pupils and sexual arousal. Whereas most of its actions are involuntary, some, such as breathing, work in tandem with the conscious mind. It is classically divided into two sub-systems, the parasympathetic nervous system and sympathetic nervous system, and it is divided into sensory (afferent) and motor (efferent) sub-systems. Within these systems there are inhibitory and excitatory synapses.

Among the neurophysiological measurements of ANS which can be used in a laboratory, there are: heart rate frequency, skin conductance and body temperature.

Using skin conductance, Damasio discovered that all subjects with frontal damages reacted just as normal subjects or like other patients with other type of brain injuries. In these subjects nothing seemed altered in the neural network which triggers skin conductance reactions.

7.7 Experiments with guessing tasks

Bechara, a student following a specialization course in Damasio's laboratory, devised a guessing task which is different from other similar experiments. Patients and normal subjects enjoy the research setting in which real life situations take place, far away from the artificial setting of typical neurophysiological tasks. Bechara wanted to be as "realistic" as possible in order to assess the decision making capabilities in a natural setting.

In the main experiment the subject is seated in front of a table on which 4 decks of cards are placed, each marked with a different letter: A, B, C and D. Subjects receive 2,000 dollars (false, but perfectly resembling true money) and are told that the aim of the game is to lose the least and try to win as much as possible.

The game consists in uncovering cards, one at a time, from any of the decks, until the experimenter stops the game; subjects do not know how many cards the experimenter will allow to turn. Each card is associated with a gain or a loss of money. Only when a card is turned is it possible to know how much the subject has earned or lost. At the beginning subjects have no way to predict what is going to happen and are not able to keep in mind the sequence of gains and losses. The game takes place, as in real life, where knowledge arrives slowly, while experience increases.

It is interesting to observe how subjects behave during the experiments. They start testing each of the decks, searching cues and regularities. Then, maybe attracted by the high gains, they show a first preference for the decks A and B which lead to higher gains but also to much higher losses, then after the first 30 cards they change strategy and start choosing decks C and D until the end of the game. Some players, who declare they like to risk occasionally go back to decks A and B, but only in order to move back to decks C and D.

Players do not have a way to perform a precise calculation of gains and losses, but gradually develop the knowledge that decks A and B are more dangerous.

Why should this test succeed where others fail? Probably because it is a good imitation of real life; it is executed in a realistic way and looks like a common card game and includes rewards and punishments expressed in money; it challenges subjects in choices aimed to obtain advantages, but it does not explain why, when and how to choose. It is full of uncertainties, but the only way to reduce them is that of producing, with any available means, guesses of probabilities, according to the fact that it is not possible to operate any precise calculation.

The behavior of patients with frontal lesions was enlightening: what they did in the test resembled what they did in everyday life after the brain damage, while it would differ from what they used to do before the brain damage. Their behavior was opposite from that of normal subjects. Patients with frontal damages, even if cooperative and paying a lot of attention to the game, chose in a disastrous way.

A lot is known about the neural networks in the damaged areas, but why does the damage of this areas block any perception of what the future consequences of choices could be?

The incredible result is that both normal subjects and patients with frontal damages produce skin conductance reactions each time they receive a gain or a loss after they turn a card. In other words, in the seconds immediately after the gain or the loss both the normal subjects and patients with frontal lesions show, through skin conductance reactions, that they have been influenced by the outcome. This is important because it tells that subjects can generate these responses in certain situations but not in others.

However in normal subjects, after they have turned a certain number of cards, something different happens. Just before they choose a card from a dangerous deck, that is to say when they have decided to choose from a risky deck, a skin conductance response is observed which increases while the game progresses. Damasio interprets this results saying that the brain learns gradually the possible negative outcome of each deck, and before a card is chosen it informs the subject through the activation of a somatic marker, which in this case can be measured using skin conductance.

The fact that subjects with neuronal damages did not show this arousal of skin conductance proves, according to Damasio, that this activation is acquired through experience, and that it increases during the conduction of the experiment, and that this somatic marker tries to inform the subject about a future outcome which could be positive or negative.

Patients with frontal injuries, on the contrary, do not show this anticipatory reaction of skin conductance, they do not show signs that their brain is learning to predict the negative outcome.

Damasio says that it is still unknown how the experiment with the cards leads to predict future outcomes. It might be that the subject develops a cognitive strategy of negative and positive outcomes and connects automatically this impression with a somatic marker which informs him about the future negative outcome which then operates as an alarm signal. In this model reasoning (a cognitive guess) precedes the somatic marker; but this is the critical point as neurological patients cannot operate "normal" decisions even though they know which are the good and bad decks.

A second model says that the somatic marker precedes reasoning. According to this model biological processes would pave the way to a rational and conscious decision. When this biological processing of information does not take place, it would be difficult to arrive at the end of the decision making process because it would require too much time and it would be insufficient to realize what is good and what is bad.

Damasio does not want to say that mind is in the body, but he only wants to state that the role of the body in brain processes is not limited to the modulation of vital functions, but it also includes information, in the way of somatic markers, which are vital for the normal functioning of reasoning.

The hypothesis of the somatic marker says that emotions mark relevant information about the future outcome of an event. Emotions produce these markers in a totally manifest way, in the form of a visceral feeling, but also using signals which cannot be consciously perceived by the brain.

7.8 Briefly

In his experiments Bechara observes 3 types of activation of skin conductance.:

1. Two activations "*after*":
   a. the positive outcome in the form of a gain;
   b. the negative outcome in the form of a loss.
2. One activation "*before*" the choice of a negative deck, and during the period in which the subject is assessing which deck to choose.

Damasio interprets this anticipated reaction of skin conductance as an effect of learning.

8

PRE-STIMULI REACTIONS
RETROCAUSALITY AND LEARNING

The experimental design used in this section allows to distinguish anticipatory effects due to learning from anticipatory effects due to retrocausality:

1. Differences in heart rate frequencies observed in phase 1, in association with unpredictable random selections operated by the computer in phase 3 can be attributed only to a *retrocausal effect*.
2. Differences in heart rate frequencies observed in phase 1, in association with the lucky/unlucky choice operated by the subject in phase 2, can be interpreted as a *learning effect*.

In this section one color has a 35% chance of being selected (lucky color), one has a 15% chance (unlucky color) and the last two colors have a 25% chance (neutral colors). The task given to the subjects is to guess the highest number of colors. Subjects don't know that colors have a different chance of being selected.

Hypotheses of this experiment are the following:

1. *Retrocausal hypothesis*: statistical significant differences in heart rate measurements are expected in phase 1 in association with target/non-target colors. These differences will be interpreted as retrocausal effects, considering the fact that the information associated with the colors quality (target or non-target) is unpredictable during the measurement of heart rates in phase 1.
2. *Learning hypothesis*: according to Damasio and Bechara (1994) a learning effect is expected in the form of heart rate differences measured in phase 1 in association with the choice (lucky and unlucky) operated by the subject in phase 2. These differences should increase in time.
3. *Interaction between retrocausal and learning effect*: the retrocausal effect and the learning effect are both assessed through heart rates

measurements; the first tests operated during the development of the software showed that the two effects interact in the form of an inhibition of the retrocausal effect by the learning effect.

The hypothesis of a possible interaction emerged during the development of the software for the execution of the experiment. Subjects involved in the first 3 experiments described (spontaneously) a "butterfly" feeling in the stomach in association with stimuli in phase 1 which would be selected by the computer in phase 3, similar to Damasio's somatic markers. In the tests carried out before starting this last experiment this feeling, this somatic marker, was not reported and the retrocausal effect showed with less strength. This element suggested the possibility of an interaction between the retrocausal and learning effect.

The same design of the first experiment was used. The difference is the selection probability of colors in phase 3: one color has a 35% chance of being selected and it is therefore the lucky color, another color has a 15% chance and is therefore the unlucky color, the last two colors have a 25% chance and are therefore neutral colors.

From a software perspective the different chances were obtained selecting randomly a number from 1 to 100.

When the number was:

1. between 1 and 35 the lucky color was shown;
2. between 36 and 50 the unlucky color was shown;
3. between 51 and 75 the first neutral color was shown;
4. between 76 and 100 the last neutral color was shown.

The same number could be selected again, making each selection totally independent.

This algorithm leads to the selection of lucky, unlucky and neutral colors in a proportion which does not coincide exactly with their theoretical probability. For example in the 3,000 trials of this experiment (30 subjects, 100 trials per subject) the lucky color was shown 36.15% times, the unlucky color 14.13% and the neutral colors 24.86%.

The experiment was conducted in the period March/April 2009. The instructions given to the experimenter were the following:

1. choose a quiet room, where the subject can be left alone for all the length of the experiment;
2. inform the subject about the total duration of the experiment (approximately 40 minutes);
3. start the recording of the heart rate frequency only after it has stabilized. Initially, heart rate frequencies are faster because of the movements that the subject makes in order to apply the heart rate measuring device. Generally speaking the stabilization of the heart rate parameter requires less than a minute from when the subject sits in front of the computer monitor for the execution of the experiment;
4. inform the subject about the task: try to guess the highest number of colors selected by the computer;
5. begin the experiment only after starting to record the heart rate frequency;
6. follow the subject for the first trial, in order to check that he/she has understood the task;
7. leave the subject alone in the room where the experiment is carried out.

At the end of each experiment the following 2 files were available:

1. the file with heart rate frequencies, produced by the software Training Monitor 2.2.0 of SUUNTO. In this file heart rate measurements are associated with the time of the measurement;
2. the file produced by the software developed in Delphi Pascal for the execution of the experiment. This file contains the exact time of presentation of stimuli (in milliseconds), exactly synchronized with the beginning of the second, the choice operated by the subject and the selection operated by the computer, associated with the characteristics of the stimuli.

As soon as the files were available, analyses were performed, in order to provide a feedback to the experimenter.

Example of retrocausal feed-back tables

	Subject n. 21					Subject n. 7			
	Blue	Green	Red	Yellow		Blue	Green	Red	Yellow
HR 1:	-0.671	2.200	-0.840	-1.103	HR 1:	0.276	-0.775	0.040	0.378
HR 2:	-0.772	2.399	-0.556	-1.471	HR 2:	0.231	-0.750	0.133	0.298
HR 3:	-0.950	2.467	-0.056	-1.766	HR 3:	0.210	-0.862	0.173	0.414
HR 4:	-1.353	2.310	1.080	-2.054	HR 4:	0.150	-0.913	0.187	0.560
HR 5:	-1.928	2.204	1.894	-1.892	HR 5:	0.117	-0.850	0.187	0.545
HR 6:	-1.954	1.897	2.474	-1.993	HR 6:	0.048	-0.875	0.227	0.640
HR 7:	-1.982	1.535	2.752	-1.755	HR 7:	-0.067	-0.688	0.320	0.491
HR 8:	-2.015	1.543	2.733	-1.704	HR 8:	-0.077	-0.763	0.373	0.524
HR 9:	-1.831	1.397	2.665	-1.704	HR 9:	-0.129	-0.712	0.427	0.482
HR 10:	-1.770	1.508	2.407	-1.691	HR 10:	-0.109	-0.700	0.467	0.375
HR 11:	-1.482	1.468	1.981	-1.641	HR 11:	-0.174	-0.625	0.467	0.402
HR 12:	-1.458	1.853	1.404	-1.637	HR 12:	-0.249	-0.650	0.600	0.378
HR 13:	-1.572	2.154	1.199	-1.679	HR 13:	-0.259	-0.625	0.573	0.402
HR 14:	-1.544	2.079	1.260	-1.676	HR 14:	-0.296	-0.525	0.573	0.348
HR 15:	-1.452	1.994	1.226	-1.661	HR 15:	-0.283	-0.513	0.507	0.405
HR 16:	-1.311	1.727	1.255	-1.541	HR 16:	-0.220	-0.525	0.413	0.438
	General total:	83.764				General total:	0.000		

The retrocausal feedback was given in the form of a table which briefly showed which were the heart rate differences associated to the target and non-target quality of the color.

The previous feedback tables shows the differences for subject 21 and subject 7. Retrocausal feedback tables consist of 16 lines, one for each of the 16 heart rate frequencies measured in phase 1. Phase 1 is repeated 100 times. It is therefore possible to calculate mean values for each color when it is target and for each color when it is non-target. The differences of these mean value provide the feedback on the retrocausal effect. For example, for subject n. 21, in the first line (HR 1), we see that the mean value of the heart rate frequencies in phase 1, when the target is blue compared to when the blue is not a target is 0,671 heart beats lower. The second line is relative to the second heart rate frequency measured during phase 1 and its value for the blue color, when target, is -0,772 heart beats per minute lower.

Retrocausal feedback tables can be represented graphically in the following way:

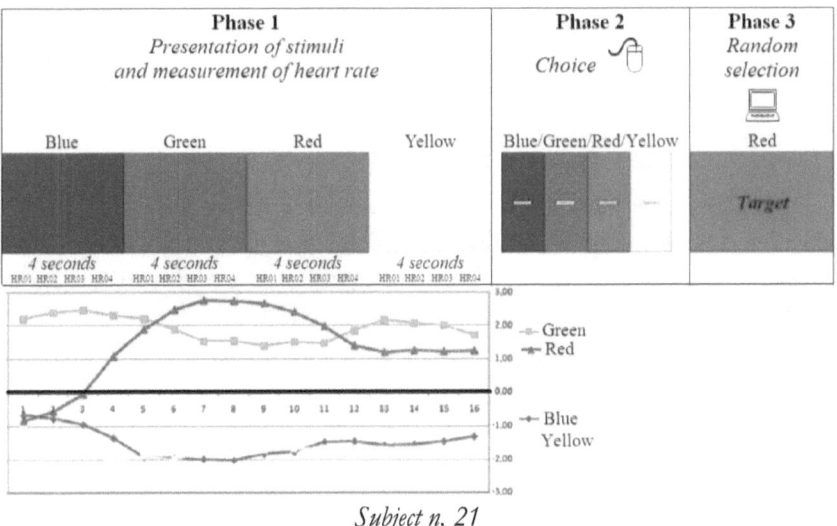

Subject n. 21

In the absence of the retrocausal effect differences should vary around the zero line (black horizontal line). We see, instead, that they diverge.

It is important to note that the effect is not limited to the presentation of the target color in phase 1, but it spreads all over phase 1. Originally, in the first three experiments, only heart rates measurements in association to the presentation of the target color in phase 1 were considered in the data analyses.

At the bottom of the retrocausal feedback tables a total value of differences is shown. This value is calculated adding only the absolute values (without negative signs), above the threshold of 1.5. In this way, casual fluctuation of data are removed from the general total. The previous feedback tables show a general total of 83,764, for subject n. 21 and a general total equal to zero for subject n. 7.

Feedback tables were used to assess if something was hindering the experiment. In the case of the first 7 subjects the effect was practically null: 4 subjects showed a general total equal to zero and 3 showed a general value lower than 15. The experiment was being conducted using an old laptop computer with a low brightness of the display. It was decided to change computer with brighter colors and a wider screen. Once this change was made, a sudden increase in the values of the retrocausal effect was observed. Using the new computer sixteen subjects showed general values of the effect over 15, three lower than 15 and five equal to zero. The number of subjects with no effect decreased from 57% to 21%.

When the total value in the retrocausal feedback tables is calculated adding the real values (with the sign) it tends to zero. This explains why the differences, comparing all targets and non-targets in the first experiment, were null, whereas when the comparison was made within each color they became statistically meaningful.

The fact that the direction of the effect can diverge and that when added together it produces a null effect, points to the inadequateness of Student's t and ANOVA. In this last experiment, data analyses were carried out using non-parametric statistical techniques, based on frequency distributions and using the Chi Square and exact test of Fisher.

Mean values in feedback tables became the raw data. Trials were divided into 3 groups: the first 33 trials (starting from the second trial), the central 33 trials and the last 33 trials. The first trial was removed from the tables. Consequently, data analyses have considered 99 trials: from the 2nd to the 100th trial.

The learning effect was analyzed using choice feedback tables.

Choice feedback tables were calculated for each subject, for each group of trial (first 33 trials, central 33 trials and last 33 trials) and were relative to each of the 16 HR measured in phase 1.

Differences of HR values were calculated in association with the choice (lucky, unlucky and neutral) operated by the subject in phase 2.

In the following example a choice feedback table is shown for subject n. 20.

Example of a choice feedback table

Subject 20 – first 33 trials				Subject 20 – last 33 trials			
Choice:	Neutral	Lucky	Unlucky	Choice:	Neutral	Lucky	Unlucky
HR 1:	-1.857	1.597	0.800	HR 1:	-0.202	3.143	-1.591
HR 2:	-1.790	1.472	0.845	HR 2:	1.136	2.507	-2.727
HR 3:	-1.070	0.722	0.675	HR 3:	1.283	2.300	-2.773
HR 4:	-0.412	0.167	0.380	HR 4:	1.577	2.121	-3.000
HR 5:	-0.055	0.181	-0.120	HR 5:	1.375	1.729	-2.545
HR 6:	0.283	0.306	-0.715	HR 6:	1.515	0.907	-2.227
HR 7:	0.577	0.056	-0.845	HR 7:	1.768	0.414	-2.227
HR 8:	0.706	0.194	-1.170	HR 8:	1.783	-0.479	-1.727
HR 9:	0.044	1.139	-1.290	HR 9:	1.669	-0.807	-1.409
HR 10:	-0.673	1.194	-0.375	HR 10:	1.915	-1.443	-1.318
HR 11:	-1.033	0.958	0.370	HR 11:	2.353	-2.136	-1.409
HR 12:	-0.912	0.500	0.700	HR 12:	2.599	-3.243	-1.045
HR 13:	-0.790	0.042	1.030	HR 13:	3.206	-3.714	-1.455
HR 14:	-0.614	-0.139	0.985	HR 14:	3.801	-4.871	-1.455
HR 15:	-0.070	-0.403	0.530	HR 15:	3.423	-4.921	-1.000
HR 16:	0.713	-0.736	-0.175	HR 16:	2.941	-4.143	-0.909
	General total:	5.244			General total:	128.018	

Values tending to zero indicate no anticipatory HR reaction previous to the choice, whereas high values (positive or negative) indicate an anticipatory reaction.

Choice feedback tables were represented graphically in the following way:

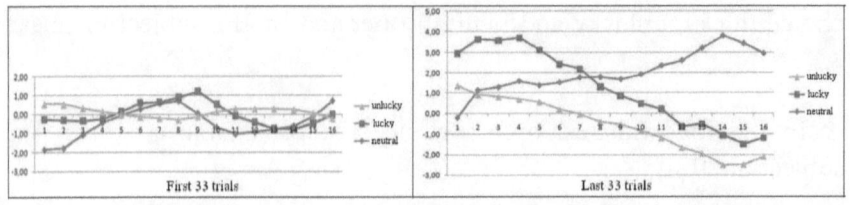

Graphical representation of the choice feedback table for subject n. 20

In this graphical representation, we see in the last 33 trials a sharp increase in the anticipatory effect, as it is expected by Damasio's learning hypothesis.

Dividing choice and feedback tables in 3 groups (first 33 trials, central 33 trials and last 33 trials), the cut off value of 1.5 does not correspond any longer to a probability error of 1% ($p < 0.01$), but it was considered as a good threshold value for the analyses.

In order to calculate Chi Square values, expected frequencies were needed.

These were obtained "empirically" using non-correlated targets (NCT): targets which are not correlated with the selection operated by the computer in phase 3.

NCT can be generated using loops, in which the first target is blue, the second green, the third red and the fourth yellow and repeating this sequence for all the 100 trials.

It was decided to use loops, since targets generated randomly produce expected frequency distributions which vary and which require the experimenter to choose among distributions.

This could lead to an artifact since a distribution which is most convenient in order to obtain statistically significant results could be chosen.

Using NCT for the production of expected frequencies, the following table was obtained for the retrocausal effect:

Frequencies	Differences of the mean values			Total
	Up to -1.500	-1.499 to +1.499	+1.500 and over	
Observed	1053 (17.83%)	3680 (63.89%)	1027 (18.28%)	5760 (100%)
Expected	781 (13.56%)	4225 (73.35%)	754 (13.09%)	5760 (100%)

Observed and expected frequencies in the distribution of mean differences of HR, measured in phase 1 in association with the selection operated by the computer in phase 3. Chi Square = 263.86

In the first group, on the left, differences up to -1.5 are associated with an observed frequency of 17.83% and an expected frequency of 13.56%; in the central class (from -1.499 to +1.499) the observed frequency is 63.89% compared to an expected frequency of 73.35%; in the last class, on the right, the observed frequency is 18.28%, the expected frequency is 13.09%. The difference between observed and expected frequencies is equal to a Chi Square value of 263.86 which, compared to 13.81 for an error probability of $p<0.001$, results to be extremely significant. It was not possible to use the exact test of Fisher as this test can be applied only to 2x2 tables.

Representing this table in a graphical way:

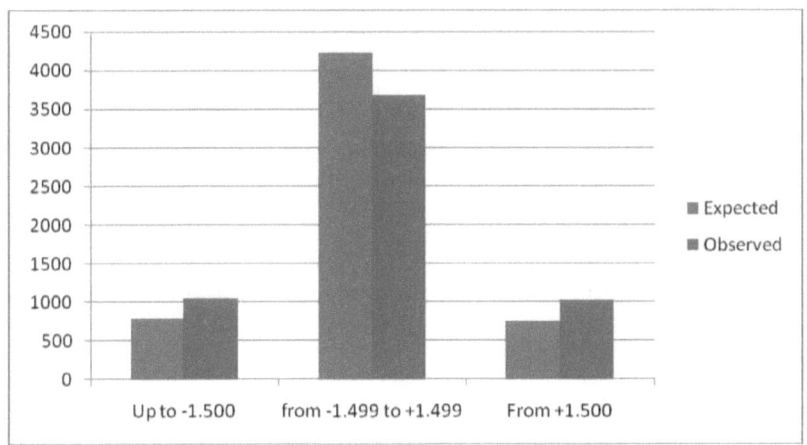

Graphical representation of the retrocausal effect

In previous experiments the retrocausal effect could be seen only on some colors which changed randomly from one experiment to the other. This was a consequence of the use of ANOVA and Student's t tests.

When the analysis is carried out using frequency distributions and non-parametric tests, the effect does not need to be additive and it is found on all the colors:

Differences	Colors				Total	N.C.T.
	Blue	Green	Red	Yellow		
From + 1.500	14.0%	22.0%	19.6%	15.7%	17.8%	13.09%
-1.499 to +1.499	60.7%	64.9%	64.6%	65.3%	63.9%	73.35%
Up to -1.500	25.3%	13.1%	15.8%	19.0%	18.3%	13.56%
	100% (n=1,440)	100% (n=1,440)	100% (n=1,440)	100% (n=1,440)	100% (n=5,760)	100.00%

Distribution of the differences of HR mean values (phase 1) associated with the selection operated by the computer (phase 3).

In this table we see for the blue color 14% of HR mean value differences over +1.5 compared to 13.09% expected (NCT column) and 24.3% under -1.5 compared to 13.56% expected.

The Chi Square value of the effect on the blue color is 176.41 equivalent to $p < 1/10^{27}$, where $/10^{27}$ indicates that before the number one 27 zeros need to be inserted.

For tables with 2 degrees of freedom Chi Square statistical significance of 0.001 (risk of committing an error when stating that the effect exists) start from the value 13.81.

For the green color the retrocausal effect is associated to a Chi Square value of 102.7, for red to a Chi Square value of 60.82 and 56.67 for the yellow color.

A graphical representation of these results is the following:

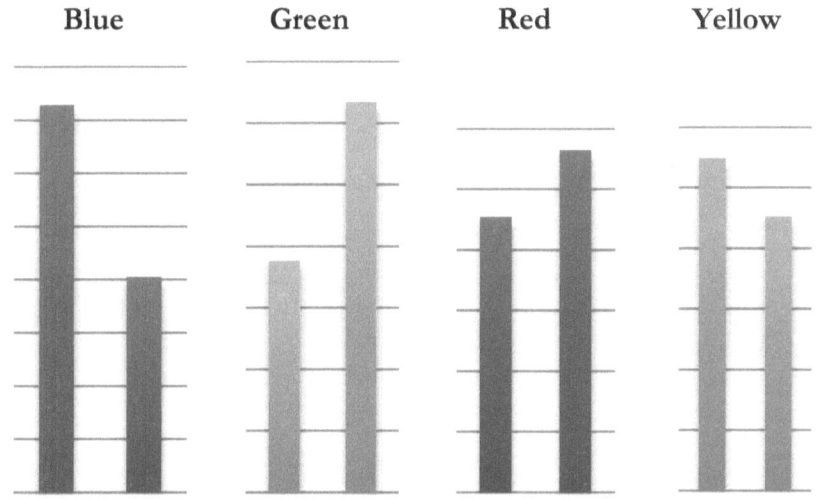

| Blue | Green | Red | Yellow |

Positive and negative differences of HR per color. Whilst on the blue color the effect prevalently takes the form of a decrease in HR and on the green color it takes the form of an increase in the HR, for red and yellow the effect is distributed in a balanced way between subjects who show an increase in HR and subjects who show a decrease in HR, becoming therefore invisible to parametric statistical analyses.

In the next tables we see how the statistical significance for colors were calculated.

The distribution of the blue color is compared with the expected distribution (NCT). The Chi Square value is 176.41 and the exact probability test shows a $p < 1/10^{27}$.

Frequencies	Differences for the blue color			Total
	Up to -1,500	-1.499 to +1.499	From 1.500	
Observed	364 (25.3%)	874 (60.7%)	202 (14.0%)	1440 (100%)
Expected	196 (13.6%)	1056 (73.3%)	188 (13.1%)	1440 (100%)

For the green color the Chi Square value is 102.7.

Frequencies	Differences for the green color			Total
	Up to -1,500	-1,499 to +1,499	From 1.500	
Observed	188 (13.1%)	935 (64.9%)	317(22.0%)	1440 (100%)
Expected	196 (13.6%)	1056 (73.3%)	188 (13.1%)	1440 (100%)

For the red color the Chi Square value is 60.62.

Frequencies	Differences for the red color			Total
	Up to -1.500	-1.499 to +1.499	From 1.500	
Observed	282 (15.8%)	931 (64.6%)	227(19.6%)	1440 (100%)
Expected	196 (13.6%)	1056 (73.3%)	188 (13.1%)	1440 (100%)

For the yellow color the Chi Square value is 56.67.

Frequencies	Differences for the yellow color			Total
	Up to -1.500	-1.499 to +1.499	From 1.500	
Observed	274 (19.0%)	940 (65.3%)	226 (15.7%)	1440 (100%)
Expected	196 (13.6%)	1056 (73.3%)	188 (13.1%)	1440 (100%)

-Learning effect

Damasio's learning hypothesis states that the choice of the subject is preceded by the activation of neurophysiological parameters of the autonomic nervous system such as skin conductance and heart rate frequencies. The learning hypothesis expects a stronger activation of the heart rate frequency in the last trials of the experiment.

Differences	Color chosen by the subject			Total	N.C.T.
	Neutral	Lucky	Unlucky		
From + 1.500	14.0%	16.6%	17.2%	16.0%	13.1%
- 1,499 to +1,499	73.5%	66.0%	66.0%	68.5%	73.3%
Up to -1,500	12.5%	17.4%	16.8%	15.5%	13.6%
	100% (n=1,440)	100% (n=1,440)	100% (n=1,440)	100% (n=4,320)	100.0%

Distribution of HR differences (phase 1) in association with the color chosen by the subject in phase 2. This table was calculate considering all the subjects and all the trials.

The observed frequencies for neutral colors coincide with the expected frequencies (73.5% compared to 73.3 expected), whereas for the lucky and unlucky colors there is a difference between observed frequencies and expected ones. This difference is associated to a Chi Square of 39.15 ($p<1/10^9$), which shows the existence of a learning effect.

The subject can choose among four colors: two neutral colors, a lucky color and an unlucky color. At the start of the experiment participants were told that colors are random. During the experiment the subject should learn the different probabilities and this would show in the form of a different activation of heart rate frequencies in phase 1, before operating the choice in phase 2.

Lucky, unlucky and neutral colors are selected randomly at the start of the experiment. During the execution of the experiment no one knows which are the lucky and unlucky colors, only at the end of the experiment this information is saved in the data file. The hypothesis is that the learning effect should increase while the experiment progresses and that it should be particularly strong in the last trials.

Differences	Trial			Total
(absolute values)	2-34	35-67	68-100	
Up to 1.499	69.4%	73.8%	62.3%	68.5%
From 1,500	30.6%	26.2%	37.7%	31.5%
	100%	100%	100%	100%
	(n=1,440)	(n=1,440)	(n=1,440)	(n=4,320)

Distribution of mean differences of HR measured in phase 1 according to the choice operated by the subject in phase 2, divided for group of trials.

The previous table shows an initial effect in the first 33 trials with a Chi Square value of 11,53, just over 0.001 of probability. In the middle 33 trials no effect is observed. In the last 33 trials the distribution differs significantly from the expected one. Chi Square value is 89,77 which corresponds to $p < 1/10^{22}$.

The following table considers only the last 33 trials of the experiment. In this table the learning effect of the lucky and unlucky colors is stronger, compared to the general table.

Differences	Color chosen by the subject			Total
	Neutral	Lucky	Unlucky	
From + 1.500	15.8%	19.2%	24.0%	19.6%
- 1.499 to +1.499	68.4%	57.7%	60.8%	62.3%
Up to -1.500	15.8%	23.1%	15.2%	18.1%
	100%	100%	100%	100%
	(n=480)	(n=480)	(n=480)	(n=1.440)

Distribution of the differences among mean HR values measured in phase 1 associated with the choice performed by the subject (phase 2). Table calculated on the last group of 33 trials, for all the subjects.

Effects are unbalanced and heart rates before the choice of the lucky color diminish whereas before the choice of the unlucky color increase. This unbalanced effect is coherent with the effect which was observed by Damasio.

It is important to note that the effect does not show in the same direction in all the subjects and it is therefore non-additive.

-Interaction between retrocausal and learning effects

In tables relative to the retrocausal effect, we see that the effect is strong in the first 33 trials, it becomes null in the middle trials and it becomes again strong in the last 33 trials. Using the exact test of Fisher, in the first 33 trials the effect is meaningful with $p < 0.76/10^{13}$, in the middle trials it practically disappears, but in the last 33 trials it turns out again to be strongly significant with $p = 0.95/10^{10}$.

Considering together the retrocausal and learning effect we see a strong retrocausal effect in the first 33 trials, whereas the learning effect is limited. Then, in the middle trials both the learning and retrocausal effect disappear. At the end of the experiment, in the last 33 trials, both effects become strongly significant.

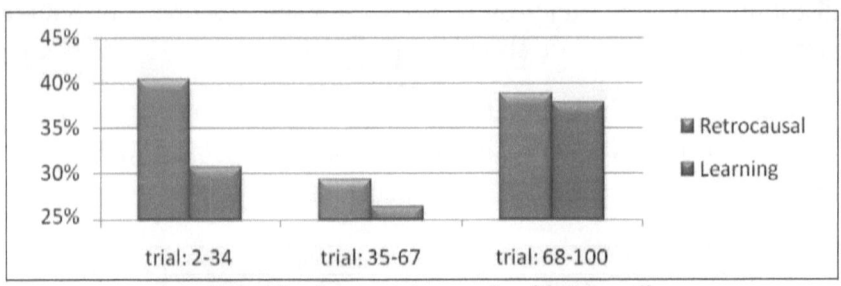

Interaction between retrocausal and learning effect.
Statistical significance of 1% starts at frequency values of 29%

The increase in the last 33 trials coincides with $p = 0,95/10^{10}$ for the retrocausal effect and $p < 1/10^{22}$ for the learning effect.

In the first 33 trials the retrocausal effect is strong, since the learning effect has not yet emerged. The two effects conflict in the middle 33 trials causing a decrease of the retrocausal effect and in the last 33 trials a strong rise in both the effects is observed.

The next table is relative to the subject with the highest values of general differences in the feedback table. The retrocausal effect is extremely strong from the beginning of the experiment, but it drastically drops in the central part of the experiment and then becomes strong again in the last trials.

Differences (absolute values)	Trial			Total
	2-34	35-67	68-100	
Up to 1.499	26.6%	67.2%	29.7%	44.0%
From 1.500	73.4%	32.8%	70.3%	56.0%
	100% (n=64)	100% (n=64)	100% (n=64)	100% (n=192)

When subjects discover the existence of a lucky color he/she could start choosing always this color, increasing in this way the correct guesses from 25% (random) to 35% of the lucky color. This increase was not observed.

In the first 33 trial the target was guessed correctly 24.75% times, in the middle trials 24.65% and in the last trials 25.47%.

This data shows that even if the learning effect is strongly visible in heart rate differences, it is not translated in the cognitive form.

9

CONCLUSIONS
THE SYNTROPIC MODEL OF CONSCIOUSNESS

Chalmers divided the problems of consciousness into:

1. The *easy problem*, which deals with the study of neurobiological models of consciousness.
2. The *hard problem* which deals with the qualitative and subjective aspects of consciousness, which escape a physicalistic and materialistic analysis.

A growing number of studies is showing pre-stimuli reactions in the parameters of skin conductance and heart rate. Anticipatory pre-stimuli reactions are neurophysiologic responses activated before the stimulus takes place.

On the basis of this evidence, Chris King suggests that consciousness arises from the constant interaction of past and future, in which two processes are active:

1. *Cognitive* (implicit and explicit), which follow the classical flow of information, from the past to the future, and which is based on the use of memory, learning and experience;
2. *Intuitive,* which follows the backwards in time flow of information, from the future to the past, and which uses the signals arriving from ANS.

Wheeler, Feynman (1949) and Fantappiè (1942) showed that advanced waves behave as absorbers whereas retarded waves behave as emitters. As a consequence of the law of syntropy, living systems behave as energy absorbers and the energy balance is therefore always be positive, in favor of absorption.

The assertion that living systems absorb energy is consistent with the fact that nearly all the energy used by humanity derives from biological masses: wood, coal, petrol, gas and bio-fuels.

The distinction between absorbers and emitters provides an interesting insight into one of the basic property of life: the *"feeling of life"*. According to Damasio the *"background feeling"* which is the equivalent of the *"feeling of life"* is the fundamental element of consciousness and life. Likewise, the background feeling of absorbing energy can be considered the essence of life itself and of the feeling of life. If this is correct, it would follow that the feeling of life, consciousness, is a direct consequence of advanced waves.

The equivalence *"feeling of life = advanced waves"* leads to the conclusion that systems based on the positive energy solution (entropy), as for example machines and computers, will never be endowed with the "feeling of life" independently from their complexity, whereas systems based on the negative energy solution (syntropy), as for example life itself, should always have a *"feeling of life"*, independently from their complexity.

In conclusion, syntropy could be the missing link between the physical world and the inner qualitative feelings.

The biologist Rosen (1985), in the book *"Anticipatory systems"* notes that:

"One of the fundamental characteristics of living beings is that of anticipating future events: It is obvious that one of the most peculiar characteristics of living systems is its dependency on future states and not only on past states."

In the volume Filters and Reflections. Perspectives on Reality published by the International Consciousness Research Laboratory (ICRL) of Princeton, a "supercausal" model of consciousness based on the hypothesis of a continuous interaction of information coming from the past and information coming from the future is suggested (Vannini and Di Corpo, 2009). According to this model the mysteries of cognitive processes, such as binding, can be explained as a consequence of the cohesive and converging properties of syntropy, which we constantly use in our daily life without being aware of it.

It is obvious that extending science to syntropy, i.e. the backward in time energy solution, results in a change of paradigm and that scientists who have proposed this change, in spite of the experimental evidences which support it, have experienced for exclusion and censorship.

Nevertheless it is also true that the only criteria which allows to distinguish between what it is true and what is false is the experimental method, the scientific method. If the scientific method supports this change of paradigm it will inevitably take form.

After four hundred years the law of syntropy is now redefining the concept of causality, adding to classical causation, which propagates from the past to the future, also retrocausality, which propagates from the future to the past.

If this is true, the consequences are simply "tremendous", not only in the field of physics, but also in biology, psychology and in life sciences in general.

10

BIBLIOGRAPHY

Amir D. Aczel (2004) Entanglement: il più grande mistero della fisica, Raffaello Cortina Editore, Milano 2004;

Anderson C.D. (1932) The apparent existence of easily deflectable positives, Science, 76:238 (1932);

Arcidiacono G. ed S. (1991) Entropia, Sintropia ed Informazione, Di Renzo Editore, Roma 1991;

Armour J.A. (2004) Cardiac neuronal hierarchy in health and disease, American journal of physiology, regulatory, integrative and comparative physiology. Aug. 2004; 287 (2), p. 262-71;

Arndt M. e Zeilinger A. (2005) Probing the limits of the quantum world, PhysicsWorld, Marzo 2005, p. 35-42;

Arntz W., Chasse B. e Vincente M. (2006) Bleep, Macro Edizioni, Cesena 2006;

Aspect A. (1982) Experimental Realization of Eintestein-Podolsky-Rosen-Bohm Gedanken-experiment, Physical Review Letters, vol. 49, 91, 1982;

Atmanspacher H., Bishop R. (2002) Between Chance and Choice, Imprint Academic, UK, p. 92.

Baaquie B., Martin F. (2005) Quantum Psyche. Quantum Field Theory of the Human Psyche, NeuroQuantology, Vol 3(1): 7-42;

Baggott J. (2003) Beyond measure, Oxford University Press, p. 171;

Bechara A., Tranel D., Damasio H. e Damasio A.R. (1996) Failure to Respond to Anticipated Future Outcomes Following Damage to Prefrontal Cortex, Cerebral Cortex, 1996, vol. 6, no. 2, p. 215;

Bechara A., Damasio H., Tranel D. e Damasio A.R. (1997) Deciding Advantageously before Knowing the Advantageous Strategy, Science, 1997, vol. 275, p. 1293;

Bechara A., Damasio H., Tranel D. e Damasio A.R. (2005) The Iowa Gambling Task and the somatic marker hypothesis: some questions and answers, Trends in Cognitive Sciences, vol. 9: 4, April 2005;

Bierman D.J. e Radin D.I. (1997) Anomalous anticipatory

response on randomized future conditions. Perceptual and Motr Skills, 84, 689-690;

Blanchard E.B., Wulfert E., Freidenberg B.M., et al. (2000) Psychophysiological Assessment of Compulsive Gamblers' Arousal to Gambling Cues: A Pilot Study, Appl. Psychophysiol. Biofeedback, 2000, vol. 25, no. 3, p. 155;

Bohm D. (1980) Wholeness and the implicate order, Routledge, Oxford 1980;

Bohm D. e Hiley B.J. (1993), The Undivided Universe, Routledge, London, p. 275-276;

Bondi M. (1998) The role of synaptic junctions in the identification of human consciousness. Biology Forum, Vol. 91: 329-334;

Bondi M. (2005) Quantum Electrodynamics and Unified Synaptic Channel in the identification of Consciousness, NeuroQuantology, Vol. 3(2): 119-133;

Capra F. (1992) Il punto di svolta, Feltrinelli, Milano 1992;

Cattell R.B. (1976) The scientific use of factor analysis in behavioral and life sciences, Plenum Press, New York 1976;

Chalmers D. (1995) Facing up to the Problem of Consciousness, in Journal of Consciousness Studies, 1995, 2, 3, pag. 201;

Chalmers D. (1996) La mente cosciente, McGraw-Hill Italia, Milano 1996;

Cleeremans A. (2003) Implicit Learning, Encyclopedia of Cognitive Science, Nature Publishing, London 2003;

Corbucci M., Iacarelli G. e Cavalieri G. (2005), Il trasmettitore a SPIN, Scienza e Conoscenza, novembre 2005, p. 16-21.

Cramer J.G. (1986) The Transactional Interpretation of Quantum Mechanics, Reviews of Modern Physics, Vol. 58: 647-688;

Cramer J.G. (2006) What's done is done… or is it?, New Scientist, 30 September 2006, pp. 6-10;

Culbertson J. (1963) The minds of robots, University of Illinois Press 1963;

Culbertson J. (1976) Sensations, memories and the flow of time, Cromwell Press, Trowbridge, UK 1976;

Damasio A.R. (1994) Descarte's Error. Emotion, Reason, and the Human Brain, Putnam Publishing, 1994;

Damasio A.R. (1999) The Feeling of What Happens. Body and Emotion in the Making of Consciousness, Heinenann, London 1999;

De Beauregard O. (1953) Comptes Rendus 236, 1632-1634;

De Beauregard O.C. (1957), Théorie synthetique de la relatività restrinte et des quanta, Gauthier – Villars, Paris 1957 ;

De Beauregard C. (1977) Time Symmetry and the Einstein Paradox, Il Nuovo Cimento (42B);

Dummett M. (1954) Can an Effect Precede its Cause, Proceedings of the Aristotelian Society (Supp. 28);

Eccles J.C. (1970), Facing reality, Springer, New York 1970;

Eccles J.C. (1989) Evolution of the brain, Routledge, Oxford 1989;

Eccles J.C. (1994) The self and its brain, Springer, Berlin, Germany 1994;

Eddignton A. (1927) The Nature of the Physical world, Ann Arbor Paperbacks, University of Michigan Press, Ann Arbor 1958;

Eddington A. (1935) New Pathways in Science. Cambridge Univ. Press 1935;

Edelman G.M. e Tononi G (2000) A Universe of Consciousness, Basic Books, 2000;

Einstein A. (1916) Relatività, esposizione divulgativa, Universale Bollati Boringhieri, Torino 1967;

Ercolani A.P., Areni A. e Leone L. (2002) Statistica per la psicologia. Statistica inferenziale e analisi dei dati, Il Mulino, Bologna 2002;

Fantappiè L. (1942) Sull'interpretazione dei potenziali anticipati della meccanica ondulatoria e su un principio di finalità che ne discende. Rend. Acc. D'Italia, n. 7, vol 4;

Fantappiè L. (1943) Teoria unitaria de la causalidad y findalidad en los fenomenos fisicos y biologicos, fundata en la mecanica ondulatoria y relativista. Rev. Mat. Hispano-Americana, s. 4, t. 3;

Fantappiè L. (1944a) Principi di una teoria unitaria del mondo fisico e biologico. Humanitas Nova, Roma 1944;

Fantappiè L (1944b) Principi di una teoria unitaria del mondo fisico e biologico, Di Renzo Editore, Roma 1991;

Fantappiè L. (1945) La nuova teoria unitaria dei fenomeni naturali. Orientamenti culturali, Roma, vol. I, f. 6, 1945;

Fantappiè L. (1947a) Visione unitaria del mondo e della vita. Conferenza, ed. Studium Christi, Roma 1947;

Fantappiè L. (1947b) Una nuova teoria unitaria, Rec. Responsabilità del Sapere, anno I, f. 1-2, Roma 1947;

Fantappiè L. (1948) Il problema sociale alla luce della nuova teoria unitaria. Responsabilità del Sapere, anno II, f. 9, Roma, 1948;

Fantappiè L. (1955a) Conferenze scelte, Di Renzo Editore, Roma 1993;

Fantappiè L. (1955b) L'eterno nel tempo, Pro Civitate Christiana, Assisi 1955;

Faye J., Scheffler U. e Urchs M. (1994). Logic and Causal Reasoning. Wiley-VCH. ISBN 3050025999;

Feynman R. (1949) The Theory of Positrons, Physical Review 76: 749;

Feynman R. (2001) Meccanica Quantistica, in La fisica di Feynman, Vol.III, Zanichelli, Bologna 2001;

Flanagan B.J. (2003) Multi-Scaling, Quantum Theory, and the Foundations of Perception, NeuroQuantology, Vol. 1(4): 404-427;

Frautschi S. (1982) Entropy in an expanding universe, Science, vol. 217, Aug. 13, 1982, 593-599;

Freeman W. (2000) Come pensa il cervello, Einaudi, Milano 2000;

Fröhlich H. (1968) Long range coherence and energy strorage in biological systems, Int. J. Quantum Chemistry, Vol2: 641-649;

Galileo Galilei (1979) Il Saggiatore, a cura di Libero Sosio, Feltrinelli, Milano 1979;

Gamow G. (1990) Trent'anni che sconvolsero la fisica, Zanichelli, Bologna 1990;

Ghirardi G.C. (2003) Un'occhiata alle carte di Dio, Il Saggiatore, Milano 2003;

Gigerenzer G (2009) Decisioni Intuitive, Raffaello Cortina Editore, Milano 2009;

Gribbin J. (2004) Q come Quanto: dizionario enciclopedico illustrato di fisica quantistica, Macro Edizioni, Cesena 2004;

Hameroff, S.R. (1982) e Watt R.C., Information processing in microtubules, J. Theor. Biol., 98:549-561;

Hameroff S.R., Penrose R. (1995) Orchestrated reduction of quantum coherence in brain microtubules: A model for consciousness. Neural Network World, Vol. 5(5): 793-804;

Hameroff S. (1998) Quantum computation in brain microtubules: the Penrose-Hameroff model of consciousness, Phil. Trans. R. Soc. Lond Vol. 356: 1869-1896;

Hameroff S. (1998) Consciousness, the brain and spacetime geometry, in The Annals of the New York Accademy of Sciences,

Special Issue Cajal and Consciousness;

Hameroff S., Penrose R. (2003) Conscious events as orchestrated space-time selections, NeuroQuantology, Vol. 1(1): 10-35;

Hameroff S. (2007) Orchestrated reduction of quantum coherence in brain microtubules, NeuroQuantology, Vol. 5(1): 1-8;

Hari S. (2008) Eccles's Psychons Could be Zero-Energy Tachyons, NeuroQuantology, Vol. 6(2): 152-160;

Herbert N. (1987) Quantum Reality: Beyond the New Physics, American Journal of Physics, Vol. 55(5): 478-479;

Herzog T. J. et al. (1995) Complementarity and the Quantum Eraser, Physics Review Letters 75 (17): 3034–3037;

Hu H. e Wu M. (2004) Spin as Primordial Self-Referential Process Driving Quantum mechanics, Spacetime Dynamics and Consciousness, NeuroQuantology, Vol. 2 (1): 41-49;

Ioannidis J.P.A. (2005), Contradicted and Initially Stronger Effects in Highly Cited Clinical Research, JAMA. 2005; 294: 218-228;

Jahn R. e Dunne B. (1997) Science of Subjective, Journal of Scientific Exploration, Vol. 11, No. 2, pp. 201–224, 1997;

James S., Spottiswoode P. e May C. (2003) Skin Conductance Prestimulus Response: Analyses, Artifacts and a Pilot Study, Journal of Scientific Exploration, Vol. 17, No. 4, pp. 617-641;

Janis I.L. e Mann L. (1977) Decision-making: a psychological analysis of conflict, choice, and commitment, New York: Free Press 1977;

Järvilehto T. (2004) Consciousness and the Ultimate Essence of Matter, NeuroQuantology, Vol. 2(3): 210-218;

Jibu M. e Yasue K. (1995) Quantum brain dynamics and consciousness, in Advances in Consciousness Research, Vol.3, John Benjamins Publishing Company, Amsterdam;

Kaivarainen A. (1992) Mesoscopic theory of matter and its interaction with light. Principles of self-organization in ice, water and biosystems, Finland: University of Turku;

Kaivarainen A. (2005) Hierarchic Model of Consciousness, NeuroQuantology, Vol. 3(3): 180-219;

King C.C. (1989) Dual-Time Supercausality, Physics Essays, Vol. 2(2): 128-151;

King C.C. (1990) Did Membrane Electrochemistry Precede Translation? Origins of Life & Evolution of the Biosphere Vol. 20: 15-25;

King C.C. (1991) Fractal and Chaotic Dynamics in the Brain, Prog Neurobiol, Vol. 36: 279-308;

King C.C. (1996a) Fractal neurodyamics and quantum chaos: Resolving the mind-brain paradox through novel biophysics, In E. Mac Cormac and M. Stamenov (Eds.), Fractals of brain, fractals of mind, Advances in Consciousness Research, 7, John Benjamin Publishing Company, Amsterdam;

King C.C. (1996b) Quantum Mechanics, Chaos and the Conscious Brain, J Mind and Behavior, Vol. 18: 155-170;

King C.C. (2003) Chaos, Quantum-transactions and Consciousness, NeuroQuantology, Vol. 1(1): 129-162;

Kuhn T. (1978) La struttura delle rivoluzioni scientifiche, Einaudi, Torino, 1978;

Laplace P.S. (1795), A philosophical Essay on Probabilities, Springer-Verlag, New York, 1995;

LeDoux J. (1996) The emotional brain: the mysterious underpinnings of emotional life, New York: Simon and Schuster 1996;

Lockwood M. (1989) Mind, brain and the quantum, Basil Blackwell, Oxford 1989;

Lorenz E. (1963) Deterministic Nonperiodic Flow, Journal of the Atmospheric Sciences, 1963, Vol.20, No.2, pp.130-140;

Lotka A.J. (1925) Elements of Physical Biology, Williams & Wilkins Co, Baltimore, reprinted in 1956 as Elements of Mathematical Biology, Dover Publications, New York;

Luisi Pier Luigi (2003) Autopoiesis: a review and a reappraisal, Naturwissenschaften, 90:49–59;

Mac Cormac E.R. e Stamenov M.I. (1996) Fractals of Brain, fractals of mind, in Advances in counsciousness research, Vol.7, John Benjamins Publishing Company, Amsterdam 1996;

Mandelbrot B.B. (1987) Gli oggetti frattali, Einaudi, Torino 1987;

Mann L. (1992) Stress, affect, and risk taking, in Risk-taking behavior (Frank YJ, ed.), pp. 202-230. Chichester: Johm Wiley & Sons 1992;

Marshall, I.N. (1989) Consciousness and Bose-Einstein Condensates, New Ideas in Psychology, Vol. 7 : 73–85;

Marshall I.N., Zohar D. (1994) Quantum Society, William Morrow, New York 1994;

Maturana H. e Varela F. (1980) Autopoiesis and Cognition: The

Realization of the Living, Boston Studies in the Philosophy of Science, vol. 42, 1985;

Maturana H e Varela F. (1984) L'albero della conoscenza, Garzanti Editore, Milano 1987;

McCratly R., Atkinson M. e Bradely R.T. (2004) Electrophysiological Evidence of Intuition: Part 1, Journal of Alternative and Complementary Medicine; 10(1): 133-143;

McCratly R., Atkinson M. e Bradely R.T. (2004) Electrophysiological Evidence of Intuition: Part 2, Journal of Alternative and Complementary Medicine; 10(2):325-336;

Mender D. (2007) Decentering the subject of physics, NeuroQuantology, Vol. 5(1): 175-181;

Monod J. (1974) Il caso e la necessità, Oscar Mondatori, Milano 1974;

Nambu Y. (1950) The Use of the Proper Time in Quantum Electrodynamics, Progress in Theoretical Physics (5);

Newton I. (1686), Principi matematici della filosofia naturale, a cura di A. Pala, UTET, Torino, 1965;

Newton I. (1704), Scritti di ottica, a cura di A. Pala, UTET, Torino 1978;

Olivetti Belardinelli M. (1991) La costruzione della realtà, Bollati Boringhieri Editore, Torino 1991;

Peijnenburg J. (1999) Shaping Your Own Life, Metaphilosophy vol. 37;

Penrose R. e Isham C. (1989) Quantum Concepts in Space & Time , Oxford University Press.1989;

Penrose R. (1989b) The Emperor's New Mind, Oxford Univ. Press 1989;

Penrose R. (1994) Ombre della mente, Rizzoli, Milano 1994;

Penrose R. (1999) The Large, the Small and the Human Mind, Carmbridge University Press, 1999, Cambridge, UK, p. 132;

Penrose R. (2005) Il grande, il piccolo e la mente umana, Cortina Editore, Milano 2005;

Penrose R. (2005b) La strada che porta alla realtà: le leggi fondamentali dell'universo, Rizzoli, Milano 2005;

Pereira A. (2003) The Quantum Mind/Classical Brain Problem, NeuroQuantology, Vol. 1(1): 94-118;

Pessa E. (1992) Intelligenza Artificiale, Bollati Boringhieri, Torino 1992;

Pitkänen M. (1990) Topological Geometrodynamics. Internal Report, HU-TFT-IR-90-4 (Helsinki University);

Pitkänen M. (2003) TGD (Topological Geometro Dynamics) Inspired Theory of Consciousness, NeuroQuantology, Vol. 1(1): 68-93;

Poli M. (1994) E. Prato Previde, Apprendere per sopravvivere, Raffaello Cortina Editore, Milano 1994;

Poincaré H (1908) Le raisonnement mathématique, in Scinece et méthode, Flammarion, Paris;

Pribram K. (1971) Languages of the Brain, Prentice Hall, New Jersey 1971;

Pribram K. (1990) Brain and Perception, Lawrence Erlbaum, Oxford 1990;

Prigatano G.P. (2003), Challenging dogma in neuropsychology and related disciplines, Archives of Clinical Neuropsychology 18 (2003) 811-825;

Prigogine I. (1979), La nuova alleanza, Longanesi Editore, Milano 1979;

Radin D. (2006), Entangled Minds, Paraview Books, New York 2006;

Reber, A.S. (1989) Implicit Learning and Tacit knowledge, Journal of Experimental Psychology: General, 118, 219-235;

Ricciardi L.M. e Umezawa H. (1967) Brain and physics of many body problems, Biological Cibernetics, Springer, Berlin, Vol. 4(2): 44-48;

Rifkin J. (1982) Entropia, Mondatori, Milano 1982;

Rosen R. (1985) Anticipatory Systems, Pergamon Press, USA 1985;

Rudfrau D., Lutz A., Cosmelli D., Lachaux J.P. e Le VanQuyen M. (2003) From autopoiesis to neurophenomenology: Francisco Varela's exploration of the biophysics of being, Biol Res 36: 27-65, 2003

Sartori L. (2004) Martinelli M., Massaccesi S. e Tressoldi P. E., Psychological correlates of ESP: heart rate differences between targets and non-targets in clairvoyance and precognition forced choice tasks, atti della Convention 2004 della Parapsychological Association, p. 407-412;

Schrödinger E. (1988) Che cos'è la vita, Sansoni, Firenze 1988;

Sharpe L., Tarrier N., Schotte D. e Spence S.H. (1995) The Role of Autonomic Arousal in Problem Gambling, Addiction, 1995, vol. 90, p. 1529;

Skarda C.A. e Freeman W.J. (1987) How brains make chaos in order to make sense of the world, Behav. Brain. Sc., vol. 10, pp. 161--195, 1987. Stuart Mill J. (1943), A System of Logic, Sistema di logica deduttiva e induttiva, UTET, Torino 1988.

Slater J.C. (1980) Teoria Quantistica della materia, Zanichelli, Bologna 1980;

Spottiswoode P. e May E. (2003), Skin Conductance Prestimulus Response: Analyses, Artifacts and a Pilot Study, Journal of Scientific Exploration, Vol. 17, No. 4, 617-641;

Stapp H.P. (1993) Mind Matter and Quantum Mechanics, Springer-Verlag, Berlin 1993;

Stapp H.P. (1999) Attention, intention, and will in quantum physics, Journal of Consciousness Studies, Vol. 6(8/9): 143-164;

Szent-Gyorgyi, A. (1977) Drive in Living Matter to Perfect Itself, Synthesis 1, Vol. 1, No. 1, 14-26;

Taylor J. (2001), Hidden Unity in Nature Laws, Cambridge University Press, 2001, Cambridge, UK, p. 337;

Szilard L. (1992) in W. Lanouette, Genius in the Shadows, Charles Scribner's Sons, New York;

Tressoldi P. E. (2005) Martinelli M., Massaccesi S., e Sartori L., Heart Rate Differences between Targets and Nontargets in Intuitive Tasks, Human Physiology, Vol. 31, No. 6, 2005, pp. 646–650;

Vannini A. (2005) Entropy and Syntropy. From Mechanical to Life Science, NeuroQuantology, vol. 3, n.2, pp. 88-110;

Vannini A. (2008) Quantum Models of Consciousness, Quantum Biosystems, 2008, 2, pp. 165-184;

Vannini A. e Di Corpo U. (2009) A Retrocausal Model of Life, in Filters and Reflections. Perspective on Reality, ICRL Press, Princeton, NJ, USA, pp. 231-244;

Varela F. (1996) Neurophenomenology: A methodological remedy for the hard problem, in Journal of Consciousness Studies, 3(4): 330-349;

Varela F., Thompson E e Rosch E. (1992) The embodied Mind, The MIT Press, Cambridge, Mass, USA;

Vitiello G. (2003) Quantum Dissipation and Information. A route to consciousness modelling, NeuroQuantology, Vol. 1(2): 266-279;

Vitiello G. (2001) My Double Unveiled – The dissipative quantum model of brain – Benjamins Publishing Co., Amsterdam 2001;

Walker E. (1970) The Nature of Consciousness, Mathematical BioSciences Vol. 7: 131—178;

Wheeler J. e Feynman R. (1945) Interaction with the Absorber as the Mechanism of Radiation, Review of Modern Physics (17);

Wheeler J.A. e Feynman R.P. (1949) Classical Electrodynamics in Terms of Direct Interparticle Action. Reviews of Modern Physics 21 (July): 425-433;

Wheeler J.A. e Tegmark M. (2001) 100 years of the quantum, Scientific American, Febbraio 2001, pp. 68-75;

Zajonic R.B. (1984) One the primacy of affect. Am Psychol 39:117-123.

BOOKS

The ASIN code is shown in brackets. It can be used to search for books if you have difficulties. The books are available in all formats. Kindle, Paper Back, Hard Cover and Audio book.

The Attractor (B0GZNHPQF9)
Introduction to Syntropy (B006QHVZPA)
Entropy and Syntropy: from mechanical to life sciences (B06XGV6XMK)
A Syntropic Model of Consciousness (B06XKKCC6F)
The balancing role of Entropy and Syntropy (B00KL4SP70)
The Unitary Theory (B01NCOVYUK)
Teilhard and Fantappiè: the converging evolution (B0H248DPN1)
Retrocausality: Experiments and Theory (B005JIN51O)
Supercausality (B005N5KLCE)
Origin of life, evolution and consciousness in the light of the law of syntropy (B005HADKWS)
The Vital Needs Theory (B006M0L0R4)
The methodology of concomitant variations (B00MOBIGWC)
World War III or Syntropy? (B0FSFC8FBT)
Apocalypse and Syntropy (B0B5RMPGKC)
Syntropy and Homeopathy (B07K5XRQNF)
Bach's flowers remedies, synchronicities and attractors (B086XBFTC1)
Climate Change (B07SRBCZVF)
Are we entering the next ice age? Will humanity survive? (B071FQLX6Z)
Syntropy the Trilogy (B09SQ5DNN7)
Money (B07S3TTS7J)
Depression (B07XGHWZ9G)
Liquidarism, Syntropy and Vital Needs (B07QDGZWPS)
Syntropy, Precognition and Retrocausality (B074W7ZL3J)
The invisible force of love (B01I4S8KV0)
The Path to Happiness (B071YWSK6K)
Colonization of Mars, Ice Age, Biological Teleportation and the Meaning of Life (B095PX92H7)